Christmas

with

Southern Living®

1990

Compiled and Edited by
Kathleen English

Oxmoor House®

©1990 by Oxmoor House, Inc.
Book Division of Southern Progress Corporation
P.O. Box 2463, Birmingham, Alabama 35201

Southern Living® is a federally registered trademark belonging to Southern Living, Inc.

Library of Congress Catalog Card Number: 84-63032
ISBN: 0-8487-1018-5
ISSN: 0747-7791
Manufactured in the United States of America
First Printing

Executive Editor: Nancy Janice Fitzpatrick
Production Manager: Jerry Higdon
Associate Production Manager: Rick Litton
Art Director: Bob Nance
Copy Chief: Mary Jean Haddin

Christmas with Southern Living 1990
Editor: Kathleen English
Assistant Editor: Margaret Allen Northen
Contributing Editor: Vicki L. Ingham
Recipe Editors: Susan Payne, Foods Editor, and Kaye Adams, Test Kitchens Director, *Southern Living*® magazine
Editorial Assistants: Laurie Anne Pate, Karen Brechin
Copy Assistant: Susan Smith Cheatham
Production Assistant: Theresa L. Beste
Artists: Barbara Ball, David Morrison
Designer: Carol Middleton

To find out how you can order *Southern Living* magazine, write to *Southern Living*®, P.O. Box C-119, Birmingham, AL 35283

Introduction 1

Christmas Around The South 2
The Grandeur of Williamsburg 4
Hanging of the Greens 10
Catch the Christmas Spirit at
   Orchard Inn 13
Angels Grace a Texas Estate 14
Dallas's Dazzling
   Display of Lights 16
Arkansas's Capital City
   Celebrates the Season 18
It's Hollyday Time at the
   Botanical Gardens 22
Quick Topiary Reindeer 24

Holiday Traditions 25
Nativities: An Inspired Collection 26
A Festive Tradition from the
   Old Country 30
Sculptor of Santas, Artisan of Angels 32
After St. Nick, They Broke the Mold 36
Christmas Comes to Dollhouses, Too 38
All You Have to Do Is Believe 40
A Crafts Tradition:
   Southwestern Style 42

Contents

Decorating for The Holidays 45

A Master Class in Classic Design.............. 46
Enduring Beauty from Living Flowers......52
Decorating with Shells and Shorebirds......54
Little Vases Lift Flowers to
    Unexpected Heights.........................56
Gold from the Garden Mixed with
    Green from the Woods.......................59
Crystalline Centerpieces............................ 60
Verve and Vitality to Suit the Season.......62
A Confection of Collections..................... 66

Christmas Bazaar 69

A Quilter's Clever Folds........................... 70
    Folded Fabric Box.................................71
Homage to England: Tartans and
    Elegant Needlework.............................. 72
    Merry Christmas Stocking..................... 72
    Merry Christmas Goose..........................72
    Tie Case..74
    Hang-Up Laundry Bag.......................... 74
    Shoe Bags...75
    Travel Picture Frame.............................75
    Sewing Kit.. 76
    Christmas Kitten Sweater.......................76
    Party Cummerbund................................ 77

Quick Tricks with Tapestry and Trims......78
Stitch a Classic Sampler Pillow.................79
Handprints in Needlepoint........................80
Bouncy Little Reindeer.............................81
A Cross-Stitch Ornament Collection.........82
    Cinnamon "Log" Carrier........................82
    A Ready Reindeer..................................83
    Dove with a Heart.................................83
Feathers, Lace, and
    Other Inspirations............................. 84
Friends Gather to Quilt.............................86
    Little Cabin Pillow............................... 86
    Little Cabin Ornament...........................87
Knitted Snowflakes and Trees...................88
Diamonds and Bands: Rich Fabric for a
    Tree Skirt..90
A Stocking Inspired
    By the Carousel..................................91
Start Something Cooking..........................92
    Green Quilted Apron.............................92
    Snowman Apron....................................94
    Stenciled Gift Tins............................... 95
Set the Table
    With Style...96
    Place Mat.. 97
    Table Runner....................................... 97
    Chair Back...98

Celebrations from The Kitchen 99

Goodies for Santa and the Kids 100
  Party Peanut Butter Sandwiches 101
  Cracker Snack Mix 102
  Fruit-and-Cheese Kabobs 102
  Simple Fruit Punch 102
  Santa's Boot Cookies 102
  Santa Claus Cupcakes 103
Around the World, Around the South 104
  Panettone 105
  Rosca de Reyes 106
  Lussekatter 107
  Letterbankets 107
  Basilopetta 108
  Mincemeat Pie 109
  Bûche de Noël 111
A New Year's Eve Extravaganza 112
  Four-Cheese Pâté 112
  Oyster-Artichoke Soup 114
  Green Salad with
    Tarragon Vinaigrette 114
  Beef Tenderloin with
    Champagne-Mustard Sauce 114
  Julienne Vegetable Sauté 115
  Sparkling Fruit Compote 115
Beverages 116
  White Christmas Punch 116
  Ruby Christmas Slush 116
  Easy Eggnog 117
  Mocha Punch 117
  Orange Wassail 117
  Marmalade Tea 117
  Hot Cranberry Sipper 117
Breads 118
  Pecan Coffee Cake 118
  Gingerbread Scones 118
  Feta Cheese Bread 121
  Sweet Potato Crescent Rolls 121
  Holiday Banana-Nut Bread 122
  Apple French Toast 122

Candies and Cookies 123
  Chocolate-Almond Pralines 123
  Chocolate-Covered Cherries 124
  Almond Fudge 124
  Brickle Dessert Wafers 124
  Almond Cookies 124
  Layered Bar Cookies 125
  Cocoa Surprise Cookies 125
  Raspberry Sandwich Cookies 126
  Chocolate-Hazelnut Sticks 127
  Blonde Brownies with Chocolate Chunks .. 127
Festive Desserts 128
  Cranberry Sherbet 128
  French Cream with Strawberry Sauce 128
  Holiday Ice Cream Bombe 130
  Festive Fruit Pie with Cinnamon Sauce .. 130
  Chocolate-Truffle Torte 130
  Coffee Soufflé Parfaits 131
  Black Walnut Spice Cake 132
  Pumpkin Pie with Spiced Cream Sauce ... 132
  Chocolate Ripple Cheesecake 133
Party Fare 134
  Sausage-Date Balls 134
  Southwestern Shrimp Mini-Tacos 134
  Antipasto Spread with Toast Rounds 134
  Bacon-Wrapped Scallops 136
  Crunchy Potato Bites 136
  Holiday Pastry Swirls 136
Gift Ideas 137
  Citrus Fruit Salad Dressing 137
  New Year's Day Chili Mix 137
  Chocolate-Almond Spread 138
  Spiced Coffee Mix 138
  Cinnamon-Nut Coffee Cake Mix 139
  Almond-Orange Bread Mix 139

Patterns 140

Contributors 156

Introduction

Everybody collects bits of Christmas memories over the years that, like the pictures in a dog-eared photo album, weave together to tell a story. Those memories become the substance of what the holiday means. And as we begin planning for the season ahead, the excitement of creating the next chapter fires the days. Who really knows what this Christmas will hold?

There are the Christmases with a new mate, in a new house, with a new addition to the family. There are the years when good fortune makes the heart swell almost to bursting, and years when sadness breaks it. And through it all, it's the people we love and the things we do to express that love in the language of the season—decorations, gifts, family gatherings, parties, and meals—that bind our lives to the meaning of the day.

This book exists to celebrate that spirit. It's designed to inspire your 1990 celebration with beauty and richness. And if it's successful, it should help create wonderful memories to add to the Christmas story you hold in your heart from year to year.

Christmas around the South

December travel offers a world of opportunities to explore the rich variety of Southern holiday celebrations. Gain inspiration from the classic decorations of Williamsburg. Experience the dazzling lights of Dallas. Journey with us as we investigate seasonal events across the South.

The Grandeur Of Williamsburg

In the 18th century, the anniversary of the birth night of the king of England was marked by a grand illumination ceremony. On this occasion, lighted candles were placed in the windows of private houses and public buildings, and fireworks lit the sky to venerate the king and celebrate his reign.

Today, Colonial Williamsburg remembers that tradition with a Grand Illumination of the city that opens the Christmas season. By sundown of the first Sunday in December, all the decorations in the historic area are in place, and an evening of entertainment by colonial dance troupes, madrigal singers, and musicians begins. A drum tattoo by the Fife and Drum Corps and a cannon salvo initiate the lighting of white candles in the windows of all buildings, and a display of 18th-century fireworks officially announces the beginning of the holiday season. Streamers, spirals, and chrysanthemum-like bursts of white light pierce the darkness around the capitol during this beautiful exhibition.

Above right: On the night of Grand Illumination, white streamers whistle and pop as fireworks ignite the month-long Christmas celebration in Colonial Williamsburg.

Right: The Great Union flag is raised at the capitol every morning—the only place in the world where it flies. The royal coronet and the monogram of Queen Anne ornament the weathervane.

Opposite: Take a carriage ride down Duke of Gloucester Street to gain a different perspective on Williamsburg. Duke of Gloucester Street is still 90 feet wide, just as originally planned, to allow for easy passage of horse-drawn traffic.

5

From the establishment of Williamsburg as the capital of the Virginia colony in 1699, the town grew and expanded, and by the beginning of the American Revolution, almost 2,000 people lived there. For 80 years, Williamsburg was the political center of the Virginia colony.

In 1780, under the governorship of Thomas Jefferson, the capital was moved to Richmond, and Williamsburg's prominence faded. Then in the 1920s, philanthropist John D. Rockefeller, Jr., pledged his financial support to the extensive project of preservation and restoration. Today, Williamsburg flourishes as a museum of living history.

During the month of December, a variety of activities, such as candlelight tours that spotlight craftsmen at work and musical performances at Bruton Parish Church, recall the festive holiday seasons of the 1770s. At dusk, visitors join character interpreters in caroling through the historic area. A candlelight ball at the Governor's Palace presents dances and music of the 18th century.

At the Powell House, visitors talk with guides portraying members of the Powell family as they prepare to celebrate the Christmas

Above left: An interpreter portraying Governor Botetourt (standing, second from left) greets his guests at an elaborate supper after the ball. On the table are some typical foods of the time, including Virginia ham and oysters. A pyramid of dried fruit makes an edible centerpiece.

Left: These musicians playing (from left to right) viola da gamba, recorder, and violin, furnish music for the colonial dancers. In 1770, the music teacher had a room on Duke of Gloucester Street where he taught music as well as the latest dances.

Opposite: The men bow, the ladies curtsey, and the dance begins. The colonial dancers, attired in their finest gowns and frock coats, whirl through reels and minuets at the ball held at the Governor's Palace on Saturday evenings during the holiday season.

8

season. The Winter Dining tour focuses on 18th-century table settings and cuisine. And of course, the Williamsburg shops offer countless opportunities for buying unique Christmas gifts. Special holiday happenings are also scheduled at Carter's Grove, Bassett Hall, and the Abby Aldrich Rockefeller Folk Art Center.

Most of the buildings in the historic area are open to visitors. Costumed character interpreters portraying Williamsburg citizens of the year 1770 lead tours on subjects ranging from architecture to gardening. These interpreters have carefully researched the lives of the people they portray and can talk about any aspect of 18th-century life.

As a living history museum, Colonial Williamsburg provides an intimate look at life in Virginia in the 1770s. In December, that historical view is enhanced by the opportunity to participate in a colonial celebration of the Christmas season.

Top right: To recapture the thrill of market days gone by, join in the auctions held every Saturday. The auction is a pleasant way to finish buying Christmas gifts or to obtain a special souvenir.

Above right: The wheelwright and other craftsmen demonstrate 18th-century methods, tools, and construction. Nightly lantern tours during December show the craftsmen preparing for the holidays.

Right: At the Powell house, visitors are expected to join in conversations with the character interpreters who portray family members. Typical of most afternoons, Mrs. Powell pours tea for her daughter while a cousin works on embroidery. Nan, the cook, serves a plate of fruit-filled tarts.

Opposite: The Governor's Palace is prominently located at the end of the palace green, just north of Duke of Gloucester Street. The original palace was completed in 1722 under Governor Spotswood, but underwent many renovations and additions over the years. Today, the buildings and furnishings reflect the year 1768 when Norborne Berkeley, Baron de Botetourt, became governor.

9

Hanging Of the Greens

Everywhere you turn in Colonial Williamsburg, you see buildings decked with fruits and greenery. The scent of fresh fruit and the sight of highly embellished wreaths envelop December visitors to Williamsburg. These elaborate decorations capture all the colors of Christmas—the many shades of greenery, red apples, pomegranates, and berries, and bright yellow lemons. Shells, feathers, pinecones, pods, and osage oranges add unusual textures to the trimmings. And the pineapple, a traditional symbol of welcome, appears often in fans and wreaths.

Each December, town residents adorn the historic buildings with 18th-century-style decorations, using only natural materials that

would have been available to colonial Virginians. Many homeowners host parties the weekend of Grand Illumination to celebrate the beginning of the Christmas season. All decorations go up that weekend, and quite often houseguests are pressed into service to help with the "hanging of the greens."

Watching this process is a good way to learn how to make these classic decorations. Many visitors return every year to delight in new combinations of materials and to gain inspiration for their own homes. A few snapshots, a quick sketch, a note of materials used, and off they go to construct their own 18th-century Williamsburg decorations.

Costumed interpreters lead daily tours describing the decorations, and workshops make possible results like those shown below. Supplies and how-to books may be ordered directly from Colonial Williamsburg (see Resources, page 155).

Catch the Christmas Spirit at Orchard Inn

If your life seems to be on fast-forward during the weeks before Christmas, come to the Orchard Inn, outside Saluda, North Carolina. You won't find cable television here. In fact, you won't even find a television. There are no whirlpool baths. And the only telephone is the one at the desk, a mahogany table with cabriole legs and a huge calendar on top. "When people call and ask about our amenities, what activities we offer," says Ann Hough, "I say, 'Books and paths.' " It's the perfect place to slow down long enough for the Christmas spirit to find you.

Ken and Ann Hough, natives of South Carolina, have operated the bed and breakfast since 1981. Ann, formerly an interior designer, furnished each of the 10 bedrooms upstairs and the living room downstairs with a comfortable combination of traditional and primitive antique pieces, oriental rugs, and framed drawings and watercolors. The kitchen became Ken's domain, where he creates original gourmet dishes as well as traditional Southern favorites—like the blueberry pancakes that are the Sunday morning standard.

At Christmas, a huge Fraser fir is the first thing you see when you enter the inn. At the base of the tree is a village of antique toys, and nearby, a group of teddy bears is having tea. Yards of fir roping swag doors, mirrors, and mantel. A fire crackles in the fireplace, and in the background, Christmas music alternates with classical pieces.

A tiny black poodle named Prissy follows Ann everywhere and helps greet guests. You sense that if you're not already a good friend, you soon will be. In fact, she says, "One of the best parts of this business is the people we've met over the years." For many visitors, the feeling is mutual, and Christmas wouldn't be the same without a night or two at the Orchard Inn. (For address and telephone number, see Resources, page 155.)

Top to bottom: Ann Hough's personal touch as hostess and Ken Hough's gourmet cooking make people want to return year after year to Orchard Inn. From the front porch, you can see the Blue Ridge Mountains to the west. At Christmas, Ken, an operatic tenor, may lead a group in caroling.

Angels Grace
A Texas Estate

Heavenly creatures flank doorways, peer from arrangements, and alight on trees throughout the lavishly decorated rooms of the DeGolyer House in Dallas, Texas. The occasion is the annual Christmas celebration, and the theme pictured here is "A Holiday of Angels."

The historic DeGolyer House, built for Mr. and Mrs. Everett L. DeGolyer in 1939, sits within the 66 acres of the Dallas Arboretum and Botanical Garden. Each year, area designers are invited to transform the rooms in keeping with the chosen theme. Then, all through December, the Dallas Arboretum and Botanical Society stages holiday activities ranging from handbell, choral, dance, and instrumental performances to piñata bashing, storytelling, and teas for area children.

Above left: Sun glints off the wings of a 14-foot angel posted at the front door of the historic DeGolyer House, situated on the grounds of the Dallas Arboretum and Botanical Garden. Berry pots make unusual luminarias.

Left: Dallas designer Howard C. Eckhart was responsible for decorating this sitting room in the DeGolyer House. A stone angel, wearing a richly hued chaplet, offers tea and refreshments. A larger wreath, studded with the same herbs and dried flowers, rests against the folds of her robe.

Opposite: In such an opulent dining room, a designer faces a formidable decorating task. Jim Bagwell rose to the occasion, with gold lamé, magnolia leaves spritzed with gold and red paint, dried flowers, feathers, and ample bunches of berries. Stone cherubs sit among the lush materials on the table, while elegant papier-mâché angels, floating in the billowing chandelier arrangement, survey the room from above.

Dallas's Dazzling Display Of Lights

It's the nation's seventh largest city, and its night skies glow with a dazzle that seems possible only in a Texas metropolis—Dallas is dressed for the holidays.

The trees wear red lights along one side of Cedar Springs Road and green along the other. The NCNB tower, the tallest building downtown, radiates its green geometry every night of the year. But looking at it down the sparkling expanse of Cedar Springs Road on a cold December night carries a magical thrill.

The Crescent Hotel ignites enormous starbursts on its two towers, and in the Lincoln Plaza, Alexander Calder's sculpture, *Man*, is joined by a glorious Christmas tree. The city lights of Dallas are a sophisticated take on the holidays, in perfect keeping with the style of the town.

Above right: Dallas's Lincoln Plaza is the site of renowned American artist Alexander Calder's sculpture, Man. *At Christmas the arched metal artwork is bathed in the glow of a glittering Christmas tree and twinkling white lights in the trees lining Akard Street.*

Right: This stunning starburst is 40 feet wide and 18 stories high. It's one of two that blaze from the towers of the Crescent Hotel. Below it, 95,000 rose-colored lights are woven into the hotel's perimeter trees.

Opposite: This view down Cedar Springs Road shows but one aspect of the drama of the city's night lights. Throughout the downtown area, trees are illuminated by twinkling lights in the colors of the season, and skyscrapers are silhouetted with bands of the same hues.

17

A tree decorated with ornaments made by Arkansas schoolchildren rises through the lower stories of the capitol's marble rotunda. Visitors to the holiday spectacle are entertained by various musical and vocal performances.

Arkansas's Capital City
Celebrates the Season

It's been over 200 years since Little Rock was a frontier town, but through all those years, it has remained the capital of Arkansas. During Christmas, government sites past and present celebrate with open houses, musical performances, and decorations galore. And state residents turn out by the thousands to revel in their history and the myriad festivities.

Arkansas's current capitol, pictured on these pages, was built in 1915 and features an enormous Christmas tree decorated with ornaments made by state schoolchildren. As visitors come each night to see it, they can enjoy live performances of holiday music. In front of the capitol, even on bitterly cold nights, Arkansans stop to contemplate a life-size Nativity carved from wood by native artist Dan Stewart.

Also celebrating the season is the Old State House, Arkansas's first state capitol. Built in the early 1800s, it is now a museum, preserving its colorful history (including fights with bowie knives—an Arkansas invention). Each year, it stages an open house with performing groups such as the Philander Smith College Choir and the Arkansas Country Dance Society. Refreshments are served in the 1836 Senate Chambers.

Above: The 230-foot dome of the capitol is covered with Arkansas limestone. During December, white lights trace its arcs and outline the building's facade. Beneath a golden star, blue lights spell PEACE.

An open house at the Territorial Restoration provides a glimpse of Arkansas's frontier days before statehood. Nearly 5,000 people tour its simply decorated exhibits, which demonstrate quilting, printing, and other early crafts. Children can make ornaments to feed the birds at the Plum Bayou Log House, and their parents can shop for handcrafted presents in the Restoration's crafts store.

At the Governor's Mansion, an open door policy admits about 30,000 people each year. An annual Christmas House Tour, staged by the Little Rock Council of Garden Clubs, features lavish decorations that epitomize the pride Arkansans have in their capital city.

Top and above: Arkansas artist Dan Stewart carved this Nativity from butternut wood. The foyer of the Governor's Mansion is decorated with poinsettias, a garland studded with dried materials, and an arrangement of leucadendron, coffee fern, alstroemeria, cedar, magnolia, heather, protea, and corkscrew willow.

Top and above: During the holidays, groups hold receptions in many of the beautifully decorated rooms of the Governor's Mansion, shown here behind its frosty fountain. In the dining room, arrangements include fresh and dried flowers, various greens, and pheasant feathers.

On the three Sunday afternoons before Christmas, Santa Claus is in the Conservatory, sitting in a poinsettia sleigh drawn by topiary reindeer.

It's HollyDay Time at The Botanical Gardens

Oranges, evergreens, cinnamon, and cloves scent the air, and the babble of children's voices rises and falls against the background of Christmas music. This happy chaos in the auditorium of the Birmingham Botanical Gardens, Birmingham, Alabama, is the children's craft workshop, HollyDay Magic. Sponsored by the Women's Auxiliary of the Birmingham Botanical Society, it is one of the Garden's liveliest holiday activities.

Projects emphasize nature and natural materials, including dried rose petals, herbs, and sprigs of pine collected from the Gardens for potpourri. Volunteers from the Junior League are stationed at every table to keep things running smoothly. A modest fee covers the cost of all supplies.

HollyDay Magic is a one-morning event, but Santa comes to the Botanical Gardens every Sunday afternoon. His sleigh, drawn by topiary reindeer, is the centerpiece of a poinsettia display in the Conservatory. An evening of caroling by candlelight is also part of the month's festivities.

Gary Gerlach, director of the Birmingham Botanical Gardens, says holiday events let people discover that there are things to see in the Botanical Gardens even in winter—deciduous hollies loaded with berries, winter-blooming shrubs, and, of course, the poinsettia display.

Above right and right: Crafts at the children's workshop include arrangements of boxwood sprigs in sandwich roll "vases." Cranberries secured with straight pins add color. Oranges dotted with cloves and rolled in cinnamon make wonderfully aromatic (but somewhat messy) pomanders.

23

Quick Topiary Reindeer

Santa's reindeer and the poinsettias surrounding them are grown by the staff at the Birmingham Botanical Gardens. The reindeer are a modern version of the ancient art of topiary. True topiary, practiced since Roman times, requires years of careful shearing to train trees and shrubs into shapes that range from formal geometrics to fanciful animals, people, and objects.

Some of the best places in the South to see such topiary are Disneyworld in Orlando, Florida; Ladew Topiary Garden, Baltimore, Maryland; and Vizcaya Museum and Gardens in Miami, Florida.

Above: Poinsettia "lips" give a whimsical look to a topiary reindeer, whose coat is teddy-bear vine growing in a sphagnum-moss base.

SANTA'S BEST FRIEND

The technique used at the Birmingham Botanical Gardens produces results that look like topiary but require much less time and effort. You start with a welded wire form, which is stuffed with sphagnum moss and then wrapped with fishing line to hold the moss in place. Forms come in a wide variety of shapes. (For mail-order information, see Resources, page 155.)

Shirley Bouchillon, horticultural specialty grower at the Botanical Gardens, explains that once the form is well stuffed, she uses hairpins to secure one- to three-inch pieces of teddy-bear vine (*Cyanotis kewensis*) to the sphagnum moss. It's important to use new growth and to lay the pieces in the same direction. For the reindeer, Shirley worked from the head down the body, following the natural pattern of deer hide.

Creeping fig and English ivy also work well. But with ivy, choose a variety with small leaves that grow close to the vine, or the leaves will be out of proportion to the shape.

Shirley soaks the form thoroughly every day. If the moss dries out, it shrinks away from the form, and the vine dies. The reindeer are kept in the greenhouse, where the warmth and humidity encourage the vines to root in four to six weeks. Gardeners can place topiary outdoors in light shade. Since high humidity is essential, place the form near a pool or on a tray of pebbles barely covered with water. Pinch back the vines whenever they grow shaggy or untidy. Your "living sculpture" should last indefinitely, as long as you keep the sphagnum moss thoroughly wet.

Holiday Traditions

Is there a moment when some special event makes Christmas seem to have really, *finally,* arrived? Most families have certain landmarks all their own that take the framework of the season and make it fit like a well-tailored suit of fur-trimmed red clothes. Share the stories of fellow Southerners who imbue the holidays with singular style through their traditions and handiwork.

Nativities: An Inspired Collection

Early in December, Mary Lois Forbes lovingly unwraps her collection of Nativity scenes and begins to arrange the figures. She has about 30 sets, which she displays throughout her beautiful old home in a historic neighborhood of Birmingham, Alabama. Mary Lois began her crèche collection about 15 years ago when her children were young.

"When Will and Tom were little, I wanted something to display that told the Christmas story," she explains. She mentioned her plan to a friend who made her a present of her first crèche, a small gold and white one, shown on page 28. Out of that simple beginning grew her extensive collection, which includes several sets from Mexico, one from Italy, and one from the Holy Land. "I became fascinated with the many styles of Nativities. Sometimes a new one I want is just a little different from one I already have," chuckles Mary Lois. She found some of her crèches while traveling and some were gifts from friends.

Mary Lois displays her collection from the beginning of Advent through Epiphany. "As I prepare for Christmas and begin to decorate, I remember past Christmases—things the boys did and the celebrations we've had. All these memories make me feel very involved with tradition," she says.

Over the years, she's refined the way she uses and cares for her collection and offers some advice. "When displaying a Nativity, be sure the Christ Child is the focus of the scene. Tuck some greenery around the figures as accents, but be careful not to overpower the scene itself," she adds. To store Nativity figures, Mary Lois recommends wrapping each figure in tissue paper and padding between them with shredded paper.

In her gift shop, Visions of Sugarplums, Mary Lois sells crèches from around the world. "A lot of Mexican ones are available here. Crèches come in a wide range of colors, sizes, and prices, making it easy to find just the right one for you." (For ordering information, see Resources on page 155.)

"The name of my shop comes from *The Night Before Christmas*. I have always loved Christmas, and my mother loved to tell me that story when I was a little girl," she recalls. "I knew I wanted to do decorations for other people, and then I saw this old house for rent in my neighborhood. So I decided to sell gift items *and* do decorating." Mary Lois has some Christmas items for sale year-round, but by the end of July almost the whole shop is devoted to Christmas.

Mary Lois believes that understanding the symbolism behind Nativity figures makes the story come alive. For example, animals are

Left: This Nativity comes from Jerusalem. The assembly of the stable roof pieces and the grain of the olive wood resemble inlay.

Above: Mary Lois Forbes sells a wide assortment of crèches in her Birmingham, Alabama, gift shop, *Visions of Sugarplums.* The large one in the middle of the table is carved from a very heavy wood native to the Philippines. At the far right is a pyramid from Germany. The rising heat from the burning candles turns the blades and makes each level of figures revolve.

Right: The intricate detail in these figures is typical of Italian Nativities. This one was produced by Anri, a 400-year-old company well-known for the beauty of its hand-carved items.

Above: Cobalt blue and stylized gold detailing distinguishes this Mexican Nativity. Ranging the figures along the mantel with just a touch of greenery is a simple and beautiful way to display a crèche. Greenery should be used sparingly to accent the Nativity figures, not overpower them.

Left: These figures from Mexico are only a few inches high. White and gold, symbolizing the purity and majesty of Jesus Christ, are common colors for Christmas decorations. Note the intricately painted flower on Mary's dress. This Nativity was the beginning of Mary Lois's collection.

used to symbolize the homage paid Christ by the humblest and least of creation. In many Nativities, a shepherd bearing a lamb is included to represent Christ as the Lamb of God. The three Magi or Wise Men are not described in detail in the Bible—their number is based on their three gifts of gold, frankincense, and myrrh. The Magi figures in Nativities are usually different ages and look as if they come from Asia, Africa, and Europe, to symbolize Christ's dominion over the world.

Some Nativities include figures from contemporary life, to illustrate the idea that God is present among the people. Native animals and everyday figures make the story more personal. In the Guatemalan crèche (*at right*), the Wise Men ride llamas, which are native to that country, instead of camels. The Mexican folk art Nativity (*below right*) includes several villagers in modern dress. One woman holds a plate with a gift of food.

Christians throughout the world celebrate the birth of Jesus Christ by arranging Nativity scenes. Many church groups stage living Nativities, complete with the creatures of the stable. In the midst of the whirl of the holidays, contemplating a crèche and recalling the first Christmas can be a meaningful experience. "Christmas is a special time for me," says Mary Lois. "I get a great sense of renewal, reflecting on the birth of Jesus. I get the feeling of a new beginning."

Above right: Mary Lois displays this Guatemalan crèche in her walnut secretary throughout the year. The artist has the Wise Men riding llamas instead of camels, because llamas are native to Guatemala. In keeping with Latin American custom, the baby Jesus is not attached to the crib, but is a separate figure. The manger is empty until Christmas Eve, when Jesus is placed in it. Jesus' hands are raised in a gesture of blessing.

Right: The primitive style of these figures, as well as the use of bright colors and modern dress, is typical of a Mexican folk art pesebre *(crib).*

29

A Festive Tradition From the Old Country

In Germany, the Christmas tree isn't just a decoration, explains Helga Missey of Acworth, Georgia. It's the centerpiece of a ceremony that celebrates family and faith. When she was growing up in Bremen, Germany, she recalls, "The tree was set up in a separate room that was closed off so that the children could not see it until Christmas Eve." The ringing of a silver bell was the signal for them to come and see the tree, laden with ornaments and lighted with white candles. "Everyone would dress up—it was a very festive occasion," says Helga. "We would read the Christmas story and each child had to recite a poem he'd learned." Then there would be presents and dinner.

Helga has raised her children in the same tradition. They are all now grown, but the

Above: Carved from craft foam, this Nutcracker greets all passersby. Helga Missey also made the straw ornaments hanging in the sidelights.

Above: In Germany, Christmas trees are customarily decorated with gold and silver ornaments. These belonged to Helga's family when she was a child.

30

Above: Collyn and Helga Missey keep Christmas in the German tradition, including the custom of decorating the tree with real candles.

candle-lit tree and a Christmas Eve meal continue to be the focus of the family celebration. "The meal in Germany varies according to region and individual family," explains Helga. "For us it's always been a cold meal: steak tartare, cold cuts, cheese and breads, smoked salmon. Then we have sweets and *Feuerzangenbowle*, a flaming punch made of Burgundy heated with cinnamon, cloves, lemon slices, and a special sugar."

When Helga and Collyn moved to Acworth from New Orleans, they wanted to do something different to mark their first Christmas there. They were looking at photos from a trip to Germany, when they came across one of a life-size Nutcracker outside a shop in Rothenberg. "Collyn said to me, 'Why don't we make one of those?'" Helga remembers. Using the photo, the couple drew a pattern. Then they carved the figure from craft foam and painted it with latex paints. Auto striping and wooden beads trim the uniform and fake fur serves as hair and beard.

"We are both creative," says Helga, "but this was our first project together, and it was a lot of fun!" Nutcracker soldiers are virtually synonymous with German Christmases, so this cheerful character brought just the right touch of the Old Country to the Misseys' new home.

Above: When the candles are lit on Christmas Eve, it's time for basking in the glow and counting blessings.

DECEMBER

Sculptor of Santas, Artisan of Angels

Pictured on these pages is the Yorktown, Virginia, gallery of folk artist Nancy Thomas. In this rambling old house, sassy seraphim and droll St. Nicks peer from cupboards and perch on tabletops, exuding the wit and humor that are this artist's trademark and, no doubt, the key to her growing popularity.

It was an early December Saturday when our editor/photographer team arrived at the gallery. Nancy and friends added finishing touches to decorations for an evening open-house party to unveil recent works. We wanted to photograph the gallery while the greenery was fresh, and before the Christmas rush depleted the shop's bounty.

Although a CLOSED sign hung on the gallery door, we had been there just minutes when Nancy's fans came rapping, hopeful that

Above right: Angels make divine folk art decorations. Amidst moon and stars, wooden angels in all shapes grace this cupboard. Some are simple cutouts; some fly from dowels; some have movable limbs. Bordering a shelf is a heavenly choir, and the heart boxes hold a celestial surprise—angels nestle within.

Below right: Folk artist Nancy Thomas—sculptor, painter, and ceramist—sits before the Boating Party sculpture in her Yorktown, Virginia, gallery.

Opposite: The jolly old elf is one of Nancy's favorite motifs. Here Cajun Santas bear gifts in small boats called pirogues and a Santa on stilts balances wreaths on a pole. There are jaunty, jointed St. Nicks of colorfully painted wood or tin, and blocky Father Christmases with grapevine crowns.

33

the perfect gifts waited within. One visitor peered into the shop and spied an angel—precisely the present she was looking for. We passed the longed-for object over our blockade of equipment and collected payment, amidst apologies for the interruption and profuse thanks and praise to Nancy.

For this modest artist, the sincerest flattery of all must come from those last-minute visitors, heading for home with gleeful good-byes and wondrous gifts for loved ones. Although Nancy has received national acclaim—she's been featured in numerous publications, her ornaments have trimmed White House Christmas trees, and her whimsical works even decorated the set of the movie *Tootsie*—it must be a heady experience, the private knowledge that on Christmas morn all across the country, your art is bringing joy. For more information about Nancy Thomas's work, see Resources on page 155.

Above left: One of Nancy's Santas, a crimson-robed gent with a cat on his head, visits this quaint cottage with the cheery painted door and the moon-and-stars roof. Boxwood topiaries landscape the festive scene.

Below left: From January's twirling ballet dancers to December's toy-haloed Santa, free association of holidays, seasonal festivities, and even astrology guided Nancy's brush for the madcap months depicted here. Painted metal cutouts—trees, birds, pumpkins—top the painted squares. On the table is Nancy's flag-blanketed horse.

Opposite: This table setting has a Peaceable Kingdom theme, with Nancy's Noah's Ark as the centerpiece and animals cavorting two-by-two along an oriental runner. Their kin serve as napkin rings. The plates—a tiger and a zebra are in the foreground—are Nancy's first ceramic designs. At the windows, bay-leaf wreaths and garlands sweeten the holiday air.

After St. Nick, They Broke The Mold

There's only one Santa Claus. And Sonja Kennedy has over 100 versions of him in her vast Christmas collection. Her home in King, North Carolina, just outside Winston-Salem, is filled with music boxes, snowballs, special edition plates, ornaments, and candle holders—even in July! She is a true Christmas devotee, living up to what a repentant Scrooge vowed to do: She honors Christmas in her heart and keeps it all the year. . . on display.

Included in her collection are the chocolate Santa molds shown on the opposite page. In arrangements, their metallic sheen stands out, and their uses extend beyond the kitchen. The chalkware Santas at left were made from chocolate molds. You can also use the molds to make candles and papier-mâché ornaments. Follow our instructions on the next page to create batches of Belsnickels (old-fashioned German Santas), Victorian Santas, and Father Christmases. For information on how to order chocolate molds, see Resources, page 155.

Above left: Sonja Kennedy of King, North Carolina, enjoys Christmas year-round. She collects ornaments, books, china, and Santas, leaving much of her collection on permanent display in her home. The molds pictured on the opposite page are from her collection.

Left: Chalkware figures like these are easy to make using chocolate molds, plaster of paris, and acrylic paints. A kindly Victorian Santa reaches into his bag of goodies, while a sterner Belsnickel looks on. (Belsnickel comes from the German Pelznickel, *meaning "St. Nicholas in fur." Belsnickels usually brought switches to naughty children, and they're often shown holding a sprig of evergreen, an ancient symbol of life amid the cold of winter.)*

MOLDING ST. NICK

To make chalkware St. Nicks, you'll need chocolate molds like these and plaster of paris, available in hardware, paint, and hobby stores.

In a clean container, mix water into plaster of paris powder, a little at a time, until plaster is the consistency of smooth, heavy paste. Stirring as little as possible, work out any lumps.

Dust a little talcum powder into the two halves of mold; then pour plaster into mold halves. Clip halves together and pour more plaster into mold through fill hole until mold is completely filled. Tap several times to remove air bubbles and prop mold with fill hole straight up. Release mold when plaster has set, usually after about an hour.

Paint Santas with acrylic paints and finish them with a coat of matte varnish.

To make candles from these molds, you'll need beeswax, candle wax, or paraffin with colored crayons and wicks (available in hardware and craft shops). Wax can be messy and hard to remove, so protect work surface with newspapers and use old non-cooking pots.

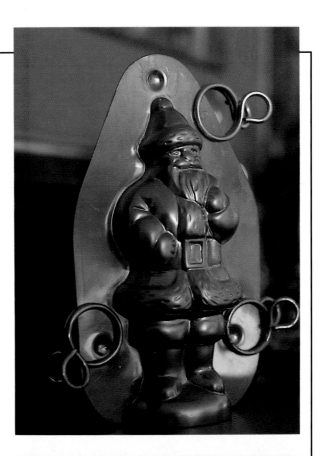

Fill pot about a third full with water, place the wax in a tin can, and set the can in the water. Heat on low to melt wax.

Place a wick through the center of the mold so that it extends out of mold on both ends. Tape two halves of mold together, to keep wax from seeping out, and clip mold halves together over tape. On end opposite fill hole, attach wick outside mold to the center of a toothpick so that toothpick is horizontal, keeping the wick taut.

When wax has melted, hold wick taut and pour wax through fill hole into mold, tapping gently on the sides to remove air bubbles. Prop mold with fill hole up and toothpick at bottom and refrigerate. As soon as the mold feels cold but before the candle has completely hardened, take the clips off and check the candle. If the wax has shrunk too much, reseal mold and pour more wax in. Continue chilling until candle has hardened.

Above: Jim and Joan McNee designed their dollhouse after a Pennsylvania farmhouse. It sits on a 110-inch-long table between the living and dining areas of their Tryon, North Carolina, home.

Christmas Comes to Dollhouses, Too

At Christmas, Jim and Joan McNee of Tryon, North Carolina, decorate two houses. But one is much smaller than the other and it always has snow for the holidays. It's a dollhouse, built to a scale of one inch to the foot and furnished with meticulous detail.

The McNees designed and built the house themselves, modeling it on the farmhouses they saw while living in Pennsylvania. They weren't aiming for architectural accuracy, but for what they considered to be typical, says Jim. Because Joan also collects anything related to elephants, the miniature farmhouse was christened Elephant Shambles. Motifs appear in every room—on the perfectly shaped valances and needlepointed rugs, in decorative objects and toys, even on the wallpaper.

Just as a real home's occupants fill it with personality, the McNees have humorously supplied this scaled-down house with a family and a story. "The original house was stucco," explains Joan McNee. "Then as the family had more money, they added a clapboard section. Later the barn was converted to a studio and playroom."

In the master bedroom, a bouquet of flowers lies on the bed "because the couple has had a squabble and he brought her roses to make up," explains Jim with a grin. An overworked nanny nods off to sleep in a rocking chair in the nursery, the son and his friends play pool in the playroom, and the cook is busy in the well-stocked kitchen.

Jim and Joan made some of the furnishings, including the petit point rugs (Joan) and the miniature folk art (Jim). But most of the furniture and accessories are pieces they've collected or received as gifts.

"The dollhouse is filled with a lot of things I'd like to have life-size and never will," says Joan. The canopy bed in the little girl's room, a prayer bench and highboy in the living room, and the dining room china are all a kind of wish fulfillment on a Lilliputian scale.

At Christmas the McNees put in a decorated tree surrounded by gifts, and they hang tiny stockings on the greenery-covered mantel. The dining table is set for turkey dinner, and in the bedroom the lady of the house wraps presents. It's a little vignette of the holidays and a source of endless delight.

Top right: The McNees built the dollhouse themselves, using the standard scale of one inch to the foot. They assembled each room as a carefully constructed vignette with its own story to tell.

Center right: The attention to detail and perfect scale make the living room seem uncannily real. Tiny stockings, greenery, toys, and tree are added just for Christmas.

Bottom right: In the bedroom, the "mother" wraps diminutive Christmas packages with brightly colored foil and ribbon.

All You Have
To Do
Is Believe

Above: Carolyn East holds four Christmas parties in the span of a week every year. She says it's easier that way, since the house is decorated and table arrangements are in place. For someone with her mix of efficiency and creativity, it probably is easier. Her dining room decorations include dozens of candles, a large hand-carved Santa, and a ficus tree strung with lights and spangled with crystal ornaments and red bows.

Top: Carolyn's handiwork shines from every nook of the living room. She covered the walls and draped the windows with paisley fabric. She also designed and crafted the stained glass windows. Santas, garlands, a Nativity, wreaths, candles, and greenery imbue the cozy room with Christmas charm.

Carolyn East missed the part where you learn what you *can't* do in life. That's why she is a landscape consultant, runs a needlepoint finishing business, operates an antique booth with a friend, and works with her husband, ministering to prisoners and troubled youths. She brings a faith and enthusiasm to her life that finds full expression at Christmastime.

"The main thing is that Jesus is the Lord of my life, and this holiday is a celebration of him. This is such a special time of year for me," she explains. "I want it to be special for other people." She decorates her Dallas home from stem to stern and then opens her doors for four parties in the span of a week every year. "We are blessed with tons of friends, and this is a little bitty house. It's wall-to-wall people, so they just come and sit on the edge of the bathtub." Thinking of it brings a chuckle. She says she once heard an eccentric described as someone who likes to make people laugh. On that score, she qualifies. The wooden cows she made for her yard have brought peals of laughter from passing children. And she probably drew smiles at the lumberyard when she asked them to tell her how to lay bricks.

"It's fun. You see, I think people can do a whole lot more than they think they can. The more you learn, the more you can do," says Carolyn. To accomplish all she wants to, Carolyn sets goals for every day. She has her Christmas shopping and wrapping done by Thanksgiving. "Sometime in the afternoon after Thanksgiving dinner, my family and I form a chain from the attic and hand down all the Christmas decorations. There are so many boxes, it takes forever!" she laughs.

But they get it done in time to observe a reverent holiday. "I guess what sustains me the most is the scripture that says, 'I can do all things through Christ.' That sizes me up best."

40

Left: One of Carolyn's many hats is that of landscape consultant, and her yard is considered one of the most beautiful in Dallas. For the holidays, her whimsically painted wooden cows pull an antique sleigh carrying a life-size stuffed Santa.

Above: Santas, dolls, teddy bears, and folk art animals from Mexico populate Carolyn's library. As part-owner of an antique booth, she has been able to fine-tune her collection by trading.

Suzanne McNeill designed and made the ragpoint Father Christmas rug on her hearth and the suede stockings with Southwestern images that hang from the mantel. For information on how to order patterns for the stockings, see Resources, page 155.

A Crafts Tradition: Southwestern Style

As Suzanne McNeill describes the handmade Christmas decorations in her home, two themes emerge time and again: the landscape of the Southwest and the inspiration she draws from her creative family.

"I always say my mother taught me everything I know, but she says she doesn't know how to do all the things I do. I tell her that she gave me the concepts." Those concepts have led Suzanne to a successful career in crafts design. She's published over 100 pattern books, covering techniques from ragpoint to painted canvas to embellished clothing. And she fills her Fort Worth home inside and out with items she's made or collected.

"I feel as if I've been doing crafts forever," Suzanne says. "When I was little, we used to make Christmas presents at home. It's a family tradition that I hope I'm passing along to my children."

To cope with busy lives, Suzanne and her sister, Brendy, have worked out a creative arrangement—each tells the other what handcrafted present she would like for Christmas. Last year, Suzanne painted a Southwestern motif on some horns and attached feathers and conchos for her sister's present. For Suzanne, her sister made a unique shirt by combining two sweatshirts with creative stitching and then adding embellishments. Each was thrilled with her gift. The women treasure their time together. "Every year, Brendy and I go with Mom to Mexico or Guatemala. That's our chance to spend time with our mother without the demands of caring for families—so we all get to be kids again!" Suzanne says.

Their visits have netted Suzanne an impressive collection of folk art. "I enjoy ethnic cultures where they do so much handwork. In Guatemala, the customs from community to

Above right: Suzanne created a lively holiday vignette for her front yard: a Texas longhorn, a jackrabbit, and cacti.

Right: Relaxing fireside with two of her children and her son's girlfriend, Suzanne and her mother leaf through a photo album containing pictures of their most recent trip to Guatemala.

43

community are different. The people wear different clothing, and their art is also different," Suzanne explains.

At Christmas, she arranges the folk art animals on her dining room table, above her mantel and along a large chest beside her stairway. She surrounds them with beautiful fabrics (some of which she designed and had printed), papier-mâché pots and hand-painted furniture by a New Mexico artist, chile pepper lights, raffia, and eucalyptus.

The stockings along the mantel are also her creations. They're made of suede, with fringed cuffs in contrasting colors. She finishes them with cutout western motifs, conchos, and thongs.

She's even creative with Christmas gatherings. In early December, she invited about 30 friends to a tree-decorating party. She prepared simple wooden cutout ornaments, all in her characteristic Southwestern style, and primed them with a base coat. Then she set out paints for her guests and watched to see what happened. "Some were very serious and sat and painted ornaments all night long. Others didn't want to paint at all—they did the tree decorating. It was fun to watch the personalities at work."

The result was a tree full of longhorns bearing the lone star of Texas, jackrabbits painted with a desert landscape, howling coyotes covered with arrows and crosses—all painted by dear friends and all enjoyed by a close-knit family.

Above left: Suzanne collects animals carved by Indians in Chichicastenango, Guatemala. For the holidays, she arranges them with raffia on her dining room table.

Left: To add spice to a Christmas party, Suzanne designed wooden cutout ornaments, primed them, and put them out with paints for her guests to decorate. Texas themes predominate: armadillos, cacti, peppers, longhorns, jackrabbits, and haciendas.

Decorating for the Holidays

A wreath hangs on the door, greenery swags the mantel, and a Christmas tree stands in its place of honor. The elements may be the same from house to house, but it's your touch that makes them a personal expression of holiday cheer. On the pages that follow, you'll find a host of bright ideas for highlighting your individual style. There are old-fashioned rock candy trees, clever ways to decorate with fresh flowers, and ideas for adding a regional accent to your decorations. And you'll find inspiration for giving a fresh, festive look to the things you live with every day.

Apples cascade along the front of this foyer arrangement, which also features huckleberry, magnolia, Foster holly, heather, pittosporum, and dried hydrangea.

A Master Class in Classic Design

Just outside of Nashville, in the community of Brentwood, Tennessee, Joe Smith strolls the frosty grounds of his 18th-century log home. He's gathering the materials he will use to decorate for the holidays. With more than 20 years of experience in floral design, he makes his selections quickly and surely: pittosporum, magnolia, holly, and heather.

"Decorating for Christmas is very simple," he says. "You just add fresh materials, a festive holiday touch, to what you live with every day—family pieces you've been given, things you've found at the antique shop. We still use things our children made in kindergarten."

Joe's philosophy is reaching an ever wider audience. He routinely lectures at such prestigious events as the Spring Garden Symposium in Williamsburg and at the National Arboretum in Washington, D.C., where he created the Living Legends Christmas program last year. His clientele has included President and Mrs. George Bush, President and Mrs. Gerald Ford, foreign diplomats, and many of Nashville's music industry luminaries.

All of them are drawn to the timeless quality of his work. Joe says, "If you stay with classics—wonderful flowers and arrangements—your decorations will always be beautiful. It goes back to the Della Robbia family in Renaissance Italy." Looking at his use of cascading apples and sliced pomegranates, one does think of the Della Robbias' glazed terra-cotta sculptures, which are still popular images for Christmas cards.

Joe's mechanics are as straightforward as his results. For the foyer arrangement with red apples, he begins with dense florists' foam. It holds more water than standard florists' foam, keeping cut materials fresh longer. He places the foam in a plastic container, taping it in place with waterproof tape. Then he fills the container with water. Wiring the apples together through their cores keeps them from

Above: The Smith's 18th-century log home sits in Brentwood, Tennessee, just outside of Nashville.

Top: Joe and Claudette Smith decorate their tree with ornaments collected over the years, including some their children made in kindergarten.

discoloring, Joe explains. He attaches them to the foam with wooden picks, which expand in the wet foam and lock in place.

For the tabletop tree in the dining room, Joe uses two blocks of foam held together with 6-inch picks. He tapes the blocks into a plastic container, going first in one direction, then in the opposite, to steady the base for the weight of the fruit. Next he trims corners off the foam to create a cone shape. Clusters of pittosporum, tightly wired to 2½-inch wooden picks, are then inserted in the foam to form the tree. Using 6-inch wooden picks, Joe attaches lemons and yellow apples to the tree in a spiral. "Pittosporum is a wonderful foliage and

Above left and above: Even with small arrangements, Joe keeps it fresh and natural—a bit of greenery, fruit, and a fallen bird's nest. For his dining room, lemons and yellow apples add spark to a tabletop tree.

48

Above right and above: To moist florists' foam in this tureen, Joe added fruit, moss, and roses, in that order. For added texture and color, he used sliced pomegranates that had been drained, cut side down, for an hour.

Above: This richly textured garland flows across an elegant bowl filled with fruit. Since the garland is so flexible, sections of it could also be curved to spiral a newel post or joined together in scallops to swag a mantel.

widely available, but you could also use boxwood," he says. "The garland of apples and lemons shows off the beauty of the greenery as well as the form of the fruit, and by using bits of holly, you get touches of red. Last, you add statice, which is a wonderful accent and retains its color as it dries."

Joe also arranges fruit and greenery on the mantel, using containers that stay there year round. He advises, "If you use color in the center of the mantel, extend it in each direction to avoid having a blob in the middle." He's an enthusiastic teacher, sharing philosophy and

techniques freely. "You can decorate any type of room, but if it doesn't have a flower or plant, especially during the holidays, it's sterile. People are spending more and more time at home between Thanksgiving and New Year's, and they are more conscious of their decorations. We're seeing an increasing emphasis on family every day. Maybe we *are* heading for a gentler nation in the nineties."

Joe Smith believes that flowers and plants are an important reflection of that trend, and his work helps bring the pleasure of beautiful arrangements to countless others.

50

FIVE STEPS TO A BOUNTIFUL GARLAND

1. Wrap moist sphagnum moss around 3 pieces of #18 wire; then wind #24 green wire around moss to secure it. **2.** Steam dried hydrangea for greater resilience. (Be careful when steaming to avoid burns.) Dip pieces in low-melt hot glue, heated in an old electric skillet set on 350 degrees, and attach to moss. **3.** Repeat to attach bay leaves and walnuts, with some of the nuts cracked open. **4.** Cluster dried roses in twos and threes for more impact. **5.** Once glue is set, garland is ready for use.

Enduring Beauty from Living Flowers

One of the best things about decorating with flowering plants is that, with surprisingly little effort and minimal expense, you can have an eye-catching centerpiece.

Frilly paper-doily collars turn the flower clusters of potted kalanchoe into a collection of nosegays. To make the collars, fold a 6-inch-wide paper doily in half, then in half again three more times, making 16 sections. Open the doily and cut along one fold; then refold accordion-style and press firmly to crease the folds. Pin or tape a collar around each flower cluster.

To make flowers as showy as giant red cyclamen the focal point of a graceful arrangement, simply place the pot in an interesting container and tuck in greenery. Candles and fruit complete the centerpiece: apples echo the color of the flowers and the coconut plays off the texture of the basket.

Forced narcissus are a holiday favorite, but the stems tend to fall over when they get too tall. To keep them upright, construct a "fence" for them to lean against. Here, branches of corkscrew willow were secured to the bottom of the container with florists' clay before the pebbles and bulbs were added. A third piece of corkscrew willow was then tied to the two vertical branches with fishing line.

When the stems are tall enough to reach the cross piece, insert pieces of ivy into the pebbles and wind the vines around the narcissus stems and the willow branches. If you force narcissus in a porous container like this terra-cotta pot, remember to place it inside a shallow glass dish or on a tray to protect wood surfaces. This second container is easy to hide with greenery and berries.

Above left: Paper-doily collars dress up two kalanchoe plants tucked into a decorated box. After the holidays, keep the plants in a sunny room and let the soil become almost dry between waterings.

Left: Cyclamen will last for months if kept in a cool room (50 to 65 degrees F) and bright, indirect light, such as that from a south-facing window.

Opposite: English ivy and corkscrew willow branches create a framework for forced narcissus and keep the stems upright. Reindeer moss covers the pebbles for a softer effect.

Decorating with Shells and Shorebirds

The festive trimmings shown here exemplify regional holiday style. With shells, shorebirds, fishnets, and oars integrated into their seasonal decorations, Tommy and Kim Mitchell bring the romance of the Chesapeake Bay inland to their Fredericksburg, Virginia, home.

You too can celebrate the distinctions of this diverse Southern region by using materials and motifs unique to your area in holiday decorations. Don't overlook the obvious: Natural materials, tools of local trades, and native folk art may be singular reflections of your locale. From seashells to tumbleweeds, duck decoys to horseshoes, there's a tremendous range of objects that can add regional flavor to your seasonal trimmings.

Above right: Merry mollusks to you. On a sea-blue door, an oyster shell wreath accented with mussel shells and the pink casings of crab shells hangs below a brass duck. Shells are attached with a hot-glue gun to a straw wreath form. Wreaths constructed in this way go together quickly, so why not gather enough materials to make extras for presents? Send a handmade regional decoration as a holiday greeting and a warm reminder of happy Christmases past to former neighbors now living in another part of the country.

Right: A grapevine wreath is studded with oyster, crab, and mussel shells for a surprising mix of textures. The windowsill holds decoys and antique wooden spools used as candle holders.

Opposite: With a few significant elements, a holiday vignette can capture the romance of a place. Here the essence of the Chesapeake Bay is summoned. In this arrangement of shoreline motifs, there's fishnet artfully draped against a brick wall, crossed oars, a mounted mallard, and holly. Greenery, wooden apple candle holders, and decoys line the mantel.

Little Vases Lift Flowers
To Unexpected Heights

Ordinarily, decorating with fresh flowers means arranging them in vases of water or containers filled with florists' foam. This tends to limit your arrangements to tabletops and mantelpieces. But with little vases, you can use cut flowers almost anywhere—on wreaths, on swags, and even on the tree.

It doesn't take many flowers to achieve a dramatic effect when you display them in such unexpected ways. And wiring miniature flower-filled containers to fir roping or a stair rail is much easier than dealing with florists' foam, chicken wire, and florists' tape. Finally, because the stems are in fresh water, the blooms will last longer than in conventional arrangements.

Specialty containers that double as Christmas ornaments offer a custom-designed look. The Santas shown here echo in miniature the pinecones wired to the newel post, and the narcissus they hold strengthen the impact of the potted bulbs placed along the steps. (The pots of narcissus help balance the visual weight of the greenery and papier-mâché bells.)

But suitable containers can also be as simple as ordinary narrow-necked medicine or perfume bottles scavenged from flea markets or your own cabinets. Or you can purchase lightweight glass vases made especially for this purpose. The ones hanging on the mantel swag (see page 58) have openings just large enough to hold a single flower: The stem itself

Above: Sprigs of holly will stay fresh much longer in the small water-filled bottles tied to this raffia-and-grapevine wreath.

Above and opposite: A Victorian-inspired Santa is both an ornament and a vase, filled with narcissus and securely wired to the garlanded stair rail.

acts as a stopper to keep the water from evaporating. To make certain the small vases are securely fastened to the garland, it's a good idea to wire them in position.

For information on how to order the vases shown here, see Resources, page 155.

Right and below: Against a background of greenery, the iridescent glass ornaments disappear and the flowers seem to float.

Gold from the Garden Mixed with Green from the Woods

Evergreens are practically synonymous with Christmas, but dried and natural materials can present an unconventional and dramatically effective alternative. Collected from the woods and the garden, mosses, branches, and flowers offer soft colors and a variety of textures, from coarse to fine. And you don't have to worry about cleaning up shedding needles or replacing withered foliage.

The mantel treatment (*at right*) starts with a nine-foot rope of sphagnum moss, purchased from a florists' supply shop. Fastened to the wall above the mirror with a small finishing nail, the roping drapes around the mirror and rests on the mantel. A honeysuckle-vine angel is attached with florists' wire to the garland, and the dried materials are then simply inserted into the sphagnum moss or placed on the mantel. (Hydrangeas, sedum, cockscomb, amaranthus, and grasses from the summer garden were air-dried in a warm attic in anticipation of Christmas decorations. Yarrow, strawflowers, bells-of-Ireland, and globe amaranth could also be dried this way.)

Because these materials have a matte appearance, the designer added a touch of sparkle by lightly spraying the tops of the hydrangeas with gold paint. Gold lamé ribbon wound loosely around the roping enhances the effect, catching the light and enlivening the arrangement. Magnolia leaves complement the tawny golds and muted greens of the dried materials.

If you can't dry your own flowers, you can buy baby's breath or German statice from a florist and use it to embellish decorations. For example, bunches of statice are simply tucked around the trio of gold papier-mâché angels (*at upper right*) to suggest snowy shrubbery. A few sprigs sprout whimsically from miniature grapevine wreaths that serve as the cherubs' halos. Shiny silver balls and gold ribbon add sparkle to the statice "bushes."

59

Sugared fruit, rock candy and snow cream trees, and oriental figures form a snow and ice scene, modeled on the 18th-century convention of arranging an edible centerpiece for a special occasion.

60

Crystalline Centerpieces

As unobtrusive as the sound of falling snow, these exquisite dinner table decorations with all-white color schemes make quiet yet dramatic statements. The magical effect belies their ease of preparation, making them especially appealing during the hectic holiday season. And the subtle beauty of the single color theme, which makes them appropriate for many decors and occasions, lies in the clever combination of various textures. Icy crystal figures contrast with waxy white tulips, and drifted snow cream trees soften brittle rock candy trees.

Snow cream trees can be made to eat the same day or to keep for about two weeks. To make the edible version, dip apple slices in sugar and use them to make a cone-shaped base for the tree. Dip a few sprigs of rosemary in egg white and then in sugar (to keep them from drying out) and insert them in the apple cone base. Mix together one quart whipping cream, four or five egg whites, and sugar to taste; whip until very stiff; and drop by spoonfuls onto the apple base. The resulting tree gives the illusion of an evergreen laden with snow drifts. For a non-edible version that will keep up to two weeks, use a craft foam cone for the base and prepare the rosemary as before, but use inexpensive whipped topping instead of the whipped cream mixture.

To make the glistening fruit cone, brush lightly whipped egg whites on apples or pears, sprinkle with sugar, and let dry overnight. Position fruit on a purchased apple cone base, adding several small branches of boxwood to fill in the gaps. (Apple cone bases are available from Colonial Williamsburg. See Resources on page 155 for ordering information.) Prepared this way, the fruit can be eaten. Or, if you wish to make a more lasting fruit cone, apply clear adhesive spray to the fruit and then sprinkle with sugar. This arrangement cannot be eaten, but it will last longer, since the adhesive spray preserves the fruit.

The inedible rock candy tree is easy to make and will last up to two years if stored carefully.

Above: Grace a formal dining room with a display of white tulips and yaupon holly in a mirrored box surrounded by a snowy scene of crystal angels and trees interspersed with snowball candles. The mirrors and crystal reflect the soft glow of candlelight, adding depth to this sparkling arrangement.

Use a hot-glue gun to attach pieces of rock candy to a craft foam cone. Store the tree in a cool place, wrapped in plastic with a few mothballs to keep insects away. If, after a time, the tree needs refreshing, simply spray it with glue and sprinkle with glitter.

Above: Peggy Pepper's home reflects her free-spirited approach to fabrics, accessories, and color. Christmas accents include potpourri in an old cigar box and a bow for the camera-loving Kitty's neck.

Verve and Vitality to Suit the Season

Peggy Pepper decks her halls with reckless abandon. After all, she's taken classes in everything from balloon-twist animals to break-dancing to wreath making since she left the oil business in favor of a more creative life.

Her energy and bold sense of style serve her well in her latest enterprise—selling one-of-a-kind fashions and accessories. And her Dallas home reflects this eclectic and independent spirit, especially during the holidays.

"When I moved to Dallas, I knew I wanted a country look. I already had this sofa—it used to be peach when I was into the 'in' colors—and I started looking at country fabrics. But most of them are muted, and I wanted to go really intense and energetic. That's when I

decided, 'Whatever my heart leaps out at is what I'm going to do, and I'm going to see how all this comes together.'"

After she found the fabric for the couch, she decided a quilt she had would be perfect on her wing chair, a Salvation Army find. Thanks to an upholstery class, she covered it herself.

"What I've done for years is, if I see something that grabs me, I buy it and set it aside until I know what I want to do with it." The coffee table is actually part of an old metal gate Peggy found. She had legs put on the gate's corners, topped it with glass, and presto chango—a customized table. For the holidays, she places an old cigar box on the table, lid raised and box filled with potpourri.

The color scheme of the living room is a natural backdrop for holiday sparkle. Around the mantel, greenery and ribbons are illuminated by candles and white lights in star reflectors.

Above: In this elegant dining room, yards of flowing fabric, greenery, and full plaid bows herald the season. Pinecones and an antique violin echo the rich tones and detailing of the mirror and buffet.

Above: Peggy's ideas can translate to any guest room—flowers, plaid pillow shams, and bed linens in holiday colors. Kitty and his sister, Kitty, (as in, "Here, Kitty, Kitty") find it comfortable.

Over the couch hangs an enormous vine wreath, crowned with greenery and paper twist ribbon. Peggy's approach to holiday decorations is not major transformation, though the results are predictably dramatic. She enhances an already strong decorating theme with arrangements that make use of her accessories. In her dining room, an exquisite old violin is the centerpiece of an opulent display. In her guest bedroom, only the colors of the bed linens and a basket of flowers evoke the holidays—nothing more is needed. This is a home that could belong to no other person. But Peggy's philosophy—following the heart's desire—is a decorating universal that is especially appropriate for Christmas.

Right: Vines, greenery, and ribbons alert visitors to what awaits them in Peggy Pepper's Dallas home.

A Confection of Collections

A collection of ornaments that grows over the years makes for a tree rich in nostalgia and tradition. But those old ornaments can take on a whole new character with the simple addition of a few "themes," such as the red bows, candy canes, and marbleized glass balls shown here. The purchased bows and candy canes are inexpensive, and you can marbleize balls yourself (see page 68). It's an easy way to recycle old glass balls that are losing their original colors or to add elegance to new ones.

And while you're giving a face-lift to tradition, instead of stacking gifts beneath the tree as usual, bring together a collection of things that evoke a sense of Christmases past. The assortment of teddy bears and Santas below this tree is arranged according to size, with the largest toward the back and the smallest in front. To provide a visual link between the bottom of the tree and the floor, Mr. and Mrs. Santa are raised on a doll table and teddy bears sit on doll chairs at the rear. All of the figures are positioned to face in the same direction, so that they seem to be welcoming everyone who enters. (This has the effect of making you want to come closer and study each one.) An old

Above: Instead of piling packages under the tree, try grouping an assortment of favorite things in a Christmassy vignette. Here, handmade and purchased teddy bears, Santas, and a variety of ornaments collected over the years line up in a cheerful display. The miniature menagerie is a creative twist on the old-fashioned villages and trains that were set up under Christmas trees earlier in this century.

Above: Adding lots of red bows, candy canes, and marbleized balls to the ornaments that go on the tree every year is an easy way to give the tree a fresh look. Repeating an element, like the bows or candy canes, also unifies an eclectic collection of tree decorations—the repetition balances the variety for a pleasing visual effect. Crocheted snowflakes, clothespin soldiers, or even glass balls in a single color can achieve a similar result.

quilt wrapped around the base of the tree hides the tree stand and provides a framework for the collection.

To create your own display, look around for collectibles that suggest childhood Christmases: Old dolls and stuffed animals arranged as if they're having tea, a toy train or old tractors and wagons, even dollhouses can become part of an appealing vignette. Books with old-fashioned illustrations or interesting covers can be stacked casually among the toys. Or fill baskets with fruit, colorful yarn, or a family of rabbits for a touch of country at the base of the tree.

HOW TO HAVE A MARBLEOUS CHRISTMAS

Marbleizing glass balls is a creative way to recycle old ornaments or to turn inexpensive new balls into handcrafted gifts. To make them, you'll need one container of water for each color of paint; oil-based enamel in the colors of your choice (red and white were used here); glass balls with hangers; and gilding powder. The containers must be deep enough to allow the ball to be completely submerged.

It's a good idea to have a clothesline handy, to hang the ornaments to dry. Be sure to spread an old shower curtain or newspapers underneath to catch dripping paint.

Place a few drops of enamel in each of the containers and swirl with a stick to create a marbleized pattern. Push the ball through the paint and into the water, slowly twisting the ball as you dip it. Then draw it out again and hang it to dry overnight. (You can speed up the process with a hair dryer.) When the first coat is dry, repeat with the same color or others to create layers of marbleized pattern. After you've applied the last coat, and while it is still wet, dust the ball with gilding powder.

This technique is so easy, you'll want to experiment. Try mixing two or three colors in the same container and swirling them for a multi-colored effect, like that on endpapers in antique books. Or let the paint on the ball dry completely. Then spray with lacquer for a higher shine and dust gilding powder into the wet lacquer.

Hang the balls with conventional hangers or, for additional glitter on the tree, tie them to the branches with gold ribbon.

Christmas Bazaar

Every year, more people are deciding that bustling crowds just won't do. Not for them, the boxes of mass-produced decorations. Instead, they make a few ornaments each year to add to a treasured collection. Their bazaar contributions are quickly turned out—almost as quickly as they're snapped up. And they fondly think of each person on their list as they craft a gift that could be for no other. Recognize yourself in any of this? Want to? Read on. This chapter is just for you.

Above: From her patchwork-embellished blouse to her sponge-painted wall, quilting authority Georgia Bonesteel surrounds herself with her craft. On her tree, folded fabric boxes hang side-by-side with patchwork ornaments.

A Quilter's Clever Folds

How else would a nationally famous quilter decorate her home except with quilts? Georgia Bonesteel, best known for her lap-quilting techniques, uses them everywhere—she even sponge-painted a patchwork pattern on her living room wall. And at Christmas, patchwork ornaments decorate her tree.

Besides designing and making quilts at her home in Hendersonville, North Carolina, Georgia writes books, hosts a television show on PBS, operates a quilt shop, and conducts workshops all over the country. She is always inventing techniques to make quilting easier, faster, and more fun. One of her innovations was the use of freezer paper to make iron-on templates for patchwork and appliqué.

For Christmas, she found another creative use for freezer paper: as the foundation for cloth boxes. Satin ribbon slipped around the sides turns the boxes into ornaments. Georgia gave her boxes away as party favors, but you could also tuck a surprise inside—potpourri, perhaps—and have an ornament elegant enough to give as a gift.

FOLDED FABRIC BOX

Materials (for one 3½″-square box):
2 (10″) squares of freezer paper
2 (10″) squares of cotton, poly-cotton blend, or rayon moiré
thread to match fabric
¾ yard (⅛″-wide) satin ribbon to match fabric

Place the shiny side of 1 piece of freezer paper on the wrong side of a fabric square. Using a dry iron on a warm setting, press the paper to the fabric. Draw diagonal lines from corner to corner on the paper to find the center of the square. Fold each of the 4 corners to the center, following Diagram 1, and press the folds with your fingers. Press each folded edge in turn to the center line as shown in Diagram 2, crease, and open again. This defines the box's base. Make cuts through both layers of fabric as shown in Diagram 3. Follow Diagram 4 to fold corners up and tuck into sides. Tack center points to bottom of box with a few stitches. Repeat to make other half of box (or lid). The lid and box can be made to the same dimensions; the lid will slip easily over the box.

To hang the box on the tree, tie ribbon around the lid, slipping the ribbon under the 2 sides with open edges. Knot ribbon at 1 corner of box, then knot the ends of the ribbon to make a loop. To make smaller boxes, cut the freezer paper and fabric into 6″ or 8″ squares.

Above: These boxes are easy to make using fabric stiffened with iron-on freezer paper. You can use any fabric that holds a crease—cotton, poly-cotton blends, moiré, and decorator chintzes work well. They make distinctive gift boxes and decorations, or ornaments for your tree.

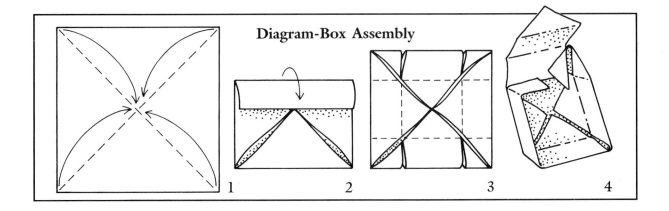

Diagram-Box Assembly

1   2   3   4

Homage to England:
Tartans and Elegant Needlework

Rolling heaths and cottage gardens, worn antiques and royal pomp and circumstance: Things British have inspired an upsurge of nostalgia in recent years often expressed in finely crafted objects for the home. The needlework collection presented here was inspired by this vogue. It offers beautiful gifts and decorations in needlepoint, knitting, appliqué, and sewing.

Tartan travel accessories and a tartan cummerbund nod to fine Scottish fabrics. A needlepointed stocking and goose wall hanging would tastefully grace cottage or castle. And a charming holiday sweater represents the time-honored tradition of fine handknitting.

MERRY CHRISTMAS STOCKING

Materials:
chart and color key on page 140
16" x 22" piece of #10 mesh canvas
2¼ yards (2"-wide) bias tape
waterproof marker
3-ply Persian yarn (see color key)
#18 tapestry needle
⅓ yard of fabric for back
⅓ yard of fabric for lining
2 yards of red piping

Note: All seams are ¼".
Zigzag-stitch bias tape to edges of canvas. Transfer design to canvas. Using all 3 plies of yarn and basketweave stitch, needlepoint design. Block needlepoint and allow to dry thoroughly. Cut out stocking, adding ¼" seam allowance.

Make pattern from needlepoint stocking, including ¼" seam allowance. Transfer to fabric for back and cut out. Transfer to fabric for lining. Cut out, reverse, and cut out. With right sides facing and raw edges aligned, stitch piping around stocking front. With right sides

facing and raw edges aligned, stitch piping to top of stocking back. With right sides facing, stitch stocking front to back on piping stitching line, leaving top open. Turn. To make hanger, remove cording from 6" of piping, turn raw edges to inside, and stitch. Loop and tack inside top back of stocking.

With right sides facing, stitch lining pieces together. Slip inside stocking, turn top edge of lining down ¼", and slipstitch to stocking around top edge.

MERRY CHRISTMAS GOOSE

Materials:
chart and color key on page 141
21" square of #10 mesh canvas
2¼" yards (2"-wide) bias tape
waterproof marker
3-ply Persian yarn (see color key)
#18 tapestry needle

Zigzag-stitch bias tape to edges of canvas. Transfer design to canvas, and using all 3 plies of yarn and basketweave stitch, needlepoint design. For goose's eye, make a double French knot. Block needlepoint and allow to dry thoroughly. Frame finished piece yourself or have professionally framed.

Opposite: Fine needlework is a legacy that has been passed along with pride from generation to generation. This holiday selection of stitchery celebrates that tradition. To exhibit your skills, choose from among a knitted sweater, a needlepointed wall hanging and stocking, an appliquéd party cummerbund, and sewn travel accessories.

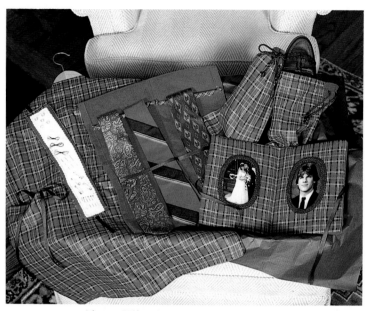

Above: Vibrant tartan is used to make a set of men's travel accessories that includes a tie case, sewing kit, hang-up laundry bag, shoe bags, and folding picture frame.

TIE CASE

Materials:
½ yard of red pinwale corduroy
2 (2″ x 10″) pieces of tartan cotton
2 (7″) lengths of ¾″ dowels
20″ (⅜″-wide) green grosgrain ribbon
thread to match fabrics
7½″ (¾″-wide) red Velcro

From corduroy, cut 1 (18″ x 17½″) piece for back and 2 (8″ x 17½″) pieces for inside panels. Fold under edges of back piece ¼″ all around and press. Fold under ¼″ on all but 1 long edge of each inside panel and press.

To make tie rods, fold 1 tartan piece in half lengthwise, with right sides facing, and stitch with a ¼″ seam along long edge. Turn and insert dowel. Repeat for second tie rod.

Stack fabrics as follows: back piece, wrong side up, and inside panels, right side up and side-by-side, with raw edges to outside and leaving 1″ of back piece extending on each

side. Place a tie rod 3″ from top across right panel, tucking ½″ of extra fabric under left panel at center of case. Cut ribbon in half. Place 1 piece 7″ from bottom across right panel, tucking ½″ under left panel in center of case. Stitch ⅛″ from inside edge of left panel from top to bottom, securing ends of tie rod casing and ribbon in seam. Flip tie rod and ribbon over on left panel and pin ends to outside left edge of case. Repeat process to attach rod casing and ribbon to center seam of right panel. (See photo.)

Topstitch ⅛″ along top and bottom edges of case through all layers. Unpin rod casings and ribbons. Fold sides of back piece over inside panels ¾″ and press. Make sure tie rods and ribbons are parallel to top and bottom of case. (See photo.) Check to be sure tension is adequate to hold ties securely, trimming fabric and ribbon if needed. Topstitch sides in place, catching ends of casings and ribbons in seams. Cut Velcro into 3 (2½″-long) pieces. Separate pieces. Stitch corresponding pieces of Velcro to top, center, and bottom of case along outside edges.

HANG-UP LAUNDRY BAG

Materials:
wooden hanger
27½″ x 22½″ piece of red pinwale corduroy
31″ x 22½″ piece of tartan cotton
thread to match fabrics
3 yards (⅜″-wide) green grosgrain ribbon

Note: All seams are ¼″.

Trace top curve of wooden hanger to make a pattern for top of bag and extend the lines equally on each side to a total width of 22½″. To make bag back, transfer pattern to a 22½″ edge of corduroy and cut out. Turn this edge under ¼″ and topstitch. Set aside.

Cut tartan into 2 (22½″ x 13¾″) pieces. To make top half of bag front, transfer pattern to a 22½″ edge of 1 tartan piece. Cut out, turn under ¼″, and topstitch top curved edge as for bag back. Turn remaining 22½" edge of this tartan piece under ¼" and press. Turn under another 1" and topstitch for hem. Repeat to hem 1 (22½") edge of other tartan piece (bottom half of bag front).

With right sides facing and curved edges aligned, pin top half of bag front to top half of bag back. With right sides facing and raw edges aligned, pin bottom half of bag front to bottom half of bag back. Hemmed edges of tartan will overlap at center. Stitch outside edges together, leaving 4" open at center top for hanger. Back-tack at each edge of hanger opening to secure. Turn.

For ties, cut ribbon into 4 equal pieces. Tack 1 end of each ribbon to top and bottom hem of tartan opening, 5" from each side. Insert hanger.

SHOE BAGS

Materials (for 6 bags):
1½ yards (36"-wide) tartan cotton
thread to match fabrics
5" x 6" piece of red pinwale corduroy
4¼ yards (¼"-diameter) green cording

Note: All seams are ¼".

For each bag, cut a 16½" x 17" piece of tartan. With wrong sides facing, fold 16½" edges together and stitch along that edge and 1 end. Turn.

For casing, fold raw edges under ¼", then another 1¼". Press and pin in place. For casing tab, cut a 2" x 2½" piece of corduroy. Fold edges under ¼" and press. Position tab on casing with 1 long edge of tab ¼" from top folded edge of bag. Unfold casing and topstitch around all sides of tab through single thickness of tartan. Snip 2 (¼") holes through corduroy tab and tartan. Refold casing and stitch to bag ⅛" from bottom edge of casing. Stitch another seam along casing ½" above first. Entering 1 hole and exiting second hole in tab, run a 25" length of cording through casing (see photograph). Knot ends of cording. Repeat to make 5 more bags.

TRAVEL PICTURE FRAME

Materials:
pattern and diagram on page 143
15½" x 11" piece of tartan cotton
15" x 9¾" piece of batting
15" x 9¾" piece of muslin
thread to match fabrics
1 yard (½"-wide) green braid
15½" x 11" piece of red pinwale corduroy
2 (7⅛" x 9⅛") pieces of cardboard
fabric glue
1 yard (⅜"-wide) green grosgrain ribbon
2 (7⅛" x 9⅛") pieces of clear acetate
2 (5" x 7") photos

Zigzag-stitch 1 (15½") edge of tartan (top edge of frame). Stack batting, then muslin, on wrong side of tartan so that tartan extends 1" on top edge and ¼" on other 3 edges. Fold side and bottom edges of tartan over muslin; whipstitch. Fold top edge over muslin; press.

Referring to Diagram, on muslin side, mark vertical center line to designate frame halves; then mark center points on each half. Transfer oval pattern to each half, aligning center marks. Machine-stitch along each oval outline through all layers. Cut out ovals, leaving ⅛" seam allowances inside stitching lines. On tartan side of frame, slipstitch braid in place to cover stitching and raw edges of ovals.

To make frame back, zigzag-stitch 1 (15½") edge of corduroy (top edge of frame). Turn under ¼" on other 3 edges and press. Turn under 1" on zigzag-stitched edge and press. Place frame front and back together, with wrong sides facing and edges aligned. Referring to Diagram, machine-stitch along vertical center of frame for fold. Slip 1 cardboard piece between front and back of each half, positioning them under top fold of frame back. Glue frame front to back along side and bottom edges.

For tie, center ribbon horizontally across back of frame and tack at center seam and sides, allowing excess ribbon to extend beyond sides of frame. Slip acetate into top of frame and position photos behind acetate. Tape photos to cardboard to hold in place.

SEWING KIT

Materials:
15½" x 4" piece of tartan cotton
13¾" x 3¾" piece of red pinwale
  corduroy
13¼" x 2¼" piece of white felt, cut to
  size with pinking shears
thread to match fabrics
21" (⅜"-wide) green grosgrain ribbon
miscellaneous sewing notions

Turn long edges of tartan under ¾" and press.
Turn ends under ¼" and press. Turn long
edges of corduroy under ½" and press. With
wrong sides facing, center corduroy on tartan.
Turn ends of tartan ½" over corduroy and
topstitch. Center felt over corduroy. Stitching
¼" from edges of felt, stitch all around
through all layers of fabric. Center green ribbon lengthwise along tartan side of kit, allowing ends of ribbon to extend beyond fabric.
Tack ribbon at 1 end of fabric and at center of
fabric. Tack or pin sewing notions to felt, fold
kit in thirds, and tie closed.

CHRISTMAS KITTEN SWEATER

Materials:
chart on page 155
sportweight mercerized cotton (50-gram
  skeins): 10 skeins red, 1 skein each
  green, white, yellow
sizes 4, 5, and 6 knitting needles (or size
  to obtain gauge)
bobbins
tapestry needle

Sizes: The directions given are for small size
(finished bust 38", finished length 22"). The
changes for medium size (finished bust 40",
finished length 23") and for large size (finished
bust 42", finished length 24") are indicated in
parentheses.
  Gauge: 5½ sts and 7½ rows = 1" in St st
on largest needles.

Note: Since it is best not to carry yarn over
more that 2 sts, it may be easier to wind yarn
on bobbins while working the chart. When
changing colors, remember to wrap old yarn
over new so that no holes occur.
  Eyelet Mock Cable Ribbing: Row 1 (wrong
side): K 2, * p 3, k 2, rep from * across. *Row 2*
(right side): P 2, * sl 1, k 2, psso, p 2, rep from
* across. *Row 3:* K 2, * p 1, yo, p 1, k 2, rep
from * across. *Row 4:* P 2, * k 3, p 2, rep from
* across.
  Back: With smallest needles and red, cast on
102 (108, 112) sts. Work in Eyelet Mock
Cable ribbing for 2½". Change to largest needles and inc 4 (4, 4) sts evenly spaced across
first row of St st. When piece measures 20"
(21", 22") from beg (ending after a k row),
change to medium-size needles, inc 1 st, and
work in Eyelet Mock Cable ribbing for 2".
Bind off all sts loosely in pattern.
  Front: With smallest needles and red, cast
on 102 (108, 112) sts. Work in Eyelet Mock
Cable ribbing for 2½". Change to largest needles and inc 4 (4, 4) sts evenly spaced across
first row of St st. Be sure to follow chart for
appropriate size. When piece measures 5"
(5½", 6") from cast-on edge, beg working
chart. When piece measures 20" (21", 22")
from beg (ending after a k row), change to
medium-size needles, inc 1 st, and work in
Eyelet Mock Cable ribbing for 2". Bind off all
sts loosely in pattern.
  Sleeves: Note: The following directions are
for ¾-length sleeves. If long sleeves are desired, cast on 5 fewer sts, then inc 5 additional
sts after Eyelet Mock Cable ribbing and work
to desired length.
  With smallest needles and red, cast on 57
(62, 62) sts. Work in Eyelet Mock Cable ribbing for 2½". Change to largest needles and
inc 12 (13, 15) sts evenly spaced across first
row of St st. If desired, continue 1 rep of
Eyelet Mock Cable pattern up the center of the
sleeve (working only 1 p before and after the 3
cabled sts). When sleeve measures 3", inc 1 st
each edge every ½", 15 (15, 16) times. When
sleeve measures 12" (12½", 13") from beg (or
desired length for long sleeves), bind off all sts
very loosely.

Finishing: Using tapestry needle and matching yarn, weave shoulder seams from armhole to neck opening for 4½" or desired length (be sure sweater will fit over wearer's head). Measure down side seams from shoulder seam 9" (9½", 9¾") and mark this point on front and back of sweater. Match center top of sleeve to shoulder seam and pin. Weave sleeve to sweater from point marked on front to point marked on back. Weave sleeve seam from wrist to underarm. Weave side seams from waist to underarm. Weave in all ends.

Standard Knitting Abbreviations:
st(s)—stitch(es)
St st—stockinette stitch (k 1 row, p 1
  row)
k—knit
p—purl
rep—repeat
sl—slip
psso—pass slipped stitch over
yo—yarn over
inc—increase
beg—begin(ning)

PARTY CUMMERBUND

Materials:
patterns on page 146
½ yard (45"-wide) red-and-green plaid
  taffeta
6" x 16" piece of thin quilt batting
4½" square of fusible interfacing
4½" square of red moiré
4½" square of paper-backed fusible web
½ yard (⅛"-wide) red satin ribbon
½ yard (⅛"-wide) green satin ribbon
red thread

Transfer cummerbund pattern to taffeta and cut 2. Cut 1 cummerbund from batting. Cut 4 (2" x 33") strips of taffeta for ties. Fuse interfacing to wrong side of moiré. Transfer heart pattern to interfacing and cut out. Following manufacturer's instructions, fuse paper-backed fusible web to wrong side of heart. Trim edges

Above: Dress up for a Christmas party with our taffeta plaid cummerbund.

even. Center heart on right side of 1 cummerbund panel. Cut each ribbon in half. Place an end of 1 red and 1 green ribbon under each side of heart as indicated on pattern. Following manufacturer's instructions, fuse heart to cummerbund.

Beginning at bottom point of heart, machine-appliqué heart with narrow satin stitch and red thread, catching ends of ribbons in stitching.

With right sides facing and raw edges aligned, stitch a tie to each end of each cummerbund piece. Press seams open. Stack pieces in the following order: batting, back (right side up), front (right side down). With ¼" seam, stitch all around, stitching ends of ties to make a point and leaving a 4" opening in the bottom seam of cummerbund for turning. Clip curves and trim batting from seam. Trim points of ties and turn right side out. Press. Slipstitch opening closed. With red thread, outline-quilt around heart, ¼" from edge.

Trim ribbons diagonally and knot ends. Tie each set of ribbons in a bow.

Quick Tricks with Tapestry and Trims

Decorating accents for the holidays don't have to involve a lot of time or trouble. Here, quick pillow make-overs and a whimsical forest of tapestry trees add striking seasonal flair.

To dress up everyday pillows, try embellishing them with bits of elegant trims. Wreaths and trees are basted on the fronts of simple shams, which can either be purchased or made envelope-style. The tasseled trims are especially effective, adding the illusion of little ornaments. Cording along the outside of the pillows, looped at the corners, provides a tailored finish.

Behind these pillows, a tapestry pillow owes its subtle sparkle to maroon and forest green braid edged in gold. Baste two rows in a diagonal swath across the pillow front, and when the holidays are over, snip the braid off without leaving a trace.

For a collection of tapestry trees, you begin with craft foam cones and remnants of tapestry or other upholstery-weight material. The fabric is folded around the cones and attached with straight pins. As shown here, tassels, cording, and braids make elegant treetoppers and garlands.

Best of all, the trees are easy to customize— tie on candies for visiting tykes, add bits of costume jewelry for sparkling ornaments and garlands, or tuck in fragrant little flowers to sweetly scent your creation. Depending on how big they are, these trees can then make striking centerpieces, mantel arrangements, or living room decorations.

Above: You can quickly transform a seating area for the holidays with decoratively trimmed pillows.

Above: Here, tapestry trees make a rich grouping when, arranged with natural materials and brass reindeer.

Stitch a Classic Sampler Pillow

The border woven into this fabric makes a striking frame for a sampler stitched in muted tones. Its sentiment extends the warmth of the season to all the days of the year.

Materials:
chart and color key on page 145
15″ square of (14-count) Dutch Garden fabric (Wichelt Imports)
embroidery floss (see color key)
15″ square of fusible interfacing
13¾″ square of fabric for back
2 (13¾″) squares of muslin
thread to match fabrics
stuffing

Note: All seams are ½″.

Center cross-stitch design on Dutch Garden fabric between textured border motif (see photograph). Using 2 strands of floss, work cross-stitch design according to chart. Use 2 strands of black-brown floss to backstitch houses and large hearts.

Fuse the interfacing to back of completed cross-stitch design. Trim the Dutch Garden fabric to 13¾″ square. With right sides facing and raw edges aligned, stitch pillow front to back around 3 sides, rounding corners slightly. Clip corners and turn.

To make pillow form, stitch muslin pieces together in the same manner. Stuff firmly and slipstitch opening closed. Insert form in pillow and slipstitch opening closed.

Above: Ornament your home with a sampler pillow. This classic cross-stitch design will complement any decor from casual to sophisticated.

Handprints in Needlepoint

Imprints of little hands capture forever the cherished memories of childhood. If you like to needlepoint, you can transform those handprints into any number of beautiful decorations and gifts—pillows, wall hangings, or cushions like this piano bench cover.

Here, each child was assigned a color for both name and handprints to make sorting the rainbow easy. Add Mom and Dad, and you have a unique family portrait.

You'll need #10 mesh canvas, acrylic paint and paint brushes, a felt-tip marker, 3-ply Persian yarn, and 2-inch bias tape. Cut a piece of canvas 4 inches wider and 4 inches longer than the desired finished size. Zigzag-stitch bias tape along the edges and mark off your design area on the canvas.

Paint a smooth layer of acrylic paint on the palms of hands and press them onto the canvas. Have each child write his or her name along the border with the felt-tip marker, or for preschoolers, print the names yourself.

Needlepoint the design, using basketweave stitch and all 3 plies of yarn. (*Note:* With #10 canvas and basketweave stitch, you'll need 48 inches of yarn for each square inch of canvas.) How you finish the piece will depend on its use. This cushion has a foam core and is backed with red cotton pinwale corduroy for durability and style.

80

Bouncy Little Reindeer

Search your scrap bag for bright cotton prints to make a herd of fabric-covered foam reindeer. This little fellow can decorate your mantel, hang on the tree, or star in a tabletop arrangement meant just for children. With a minimum of supervision, older children could even help fashion the reindeer. And since it's so easy to make, it's perfect for a bazaar.

Materials:
pattern on page 146
6" x 7" piece of 1"-thick foam
craft knife
12" x 7" piece of fusible interfacing
12" x 7" piece of red cotton print
liquid ravel preventer
threads: black, red
27" (1"-wide) red grosgrain ribbon
6½" (⅝"-wide) green-and-red grosgrain ribbon

Aligning bottom of feet with straight edge of foam, transfer pattern to foam and cut out, using craft knife with a new blade. (Cut slowly with straight up-and-down sawing motions, to avoid ripping the foam.)

Fuse interfacing to wrong side of fabric. Adding ¼" seam allowance, transfer pattern to fabric and cut out reindeer front and back. (*Note:* Cut in a little closer than ¼" at neck and antlers to define shape. If necessary, place a drop of liquid ravel preventer at these points.) Referring to pattern for placement, satin-stitch eye on front and back with black thread. Clip curves and corners. Turn seam allowance to wrong side and baste.

Place 1 fabric reindeer on matching side of foam reindeer and pin. Beginning near bottom of back leg, pin 1"-wide ribbon around edge of reindeer, overlapping ends. Turn under ¼" at end of ribbon and slipstitch ends together. With red thread, slipstitch folded fabric edge to ribbon edge all around. Repeat to stitch remaining fabric reindeer to other side of foam. Referring to photograph for placement, wrap ⅝"-wide ribbon around middle of reindeer, overlapping ends on tummy. Turn under ¼" and slipstitch ends together.

A Cross-Stitch Ornament Collection

These cross-stitch ornaments will fill many holiday needs—package toppers, bazaar items, additions to ever-growing collections—and take only a blink to make.

Our little reindeer is keeping a vigil over Santa's wash. Fragrant cinnamon sticks serve as the "logs" and baby's breath as the "kindling" in a homespun carrier that bears a touching bit of holiday wisdom. And our plump dove wears his heart (the only cross-stitching) on his wing. A special woven fabric provides the rest of his coloration.

CINNAMON "LOG" CARRIER

Materials (for 1 ornament):
chart and color key on page 142
2½" x 8" piece of (14-count) Fiddler's
cloth
liquid ravel preventer
embroidery floss (see color key)
craft glue
9" (⅛"-wide) red satin ribbon
2 (4"-long) cinnamon sticks
small bunch of baby's breath

Apply liquid ravel preventer to all edges of Fiddler's cloth. Fold cloth in half to measure 2½" x 4". Center design on top half of cloth, with top of design about ¾" from top edge of cloth. Using 2 strands of floss, work cross-stitch design according to chart. Use 1 strand of red to backstitch letters. Overlap ends of fabric ¼" and glue, forming a tube. For hanger, glue ends of ribbon to wrong side at opposite ends of carrier top. Insert cinnamon sticks and baby's breath in bottom of carrier and glue in place (see photograph).

A READY REINDEER

Materials (for 1 ornament):
chart and color key on page 143
4″ square of (22-count) ivory Hardanger cloth
embroidery floss (see color key)
#26 tapestry needle
3″-diameter circle of cardboard
hot-glue gun and glue sticks
4″-diameter reed wreath
24″ (⅛″-wide) green satin ribbon
15″ (⅛″-wide) red satin ribbon

Using 1 strand of floss, center and work cross-stitch design on Hardanger cloth according to chart. Use 1 strand of black floss to backstitch all details and to make French knot for eye. Use 1 strand of green to backstitch letters and numbers. Use 1 strand of red to make a small bow for wreath around reindeer's neck.

Centering design, glue wrong side of cross-stitched piece to cardboard. Trim fabric even with edges of cardboard. Glue wreath to outside edges on right side of ornament. Cut a 15″ length of green ribbon. Hold green and red ribbons together and tie in a bow. Glue bow to top of wreath, arranging and gluing tails in place as shown in photograph. To make hanger, fold remaining green ribbon in half and glue ends to back of ornament at top.

DOVE WITH A HEART

Materials (for 2 birds):
chart and patterns on page 143
15″ square of (14-count) Charles Craft Corner Block fabric in plum/teal/smoke
DMC #601 Rose embroidery floss
15″ square of muslin (for back)
2 (12″) pieces of ivory pearl cotton thread (for hangers)
stuffing
2 (½″) dark green buttons
threads: ecru, dark green

Note: Add ¼″ seam allowance to patterns. All seams are ¼″.

Transfer body pattern to cross-stitch fabric with body over plaid area and head on natural area. Transfer wing pattern to natural area. Using 2 strands of floss, cross-stitch heart on wing, following chart.

Cut out body and wing. Transfer patterns to muslin and cut out for back.

Fold 1 piece of ivory pearl cotton thread in half. With raw edges aligned and loop to inside, pin ends to right side of bird back where indicated on pattern. With right sides facing and raw edges aligned, stitch front and back together, leaving open where indicated on pattern. Clip curves and corners and turn. Stuff firmly. Slipstitch opening closed. Complete wing in the same manner.

Referring to pattern, with ecru thread, quilt along quilting lines on tail and wing. Slipstitch wing to body as shown on pattern. With dark green thread, attach button for eye. Repeat for second bird ornament.

Feathers, Lace, and Other Inspirations

Feathers and pressed leaves, bits of ribbon and lace, pieces of art paper in favorite hues—perhaps you tuck away things like these as they catch your fancy. If so, bring them out for a holiday workshop one quiet early-winter afternoon, and make cards, wraps, and boxes like those shown here.

If you begin collecting with Christmas possibilities in mind, you'll have a bounty of materials when the season arrives. Gather and dry summer grasses and flowers. Press autumn leaves in wax paper between the pages of an old phone book. Save extra lace, ribbon, and cording from sewing and home decorating projects. Collect favorite images from old cards and visit an art supply store to select small sheets of textured stock. Pay special attention to the way colors, textures, and patterns play against each other.

You can choose from among the many types of paints now available and then use leaves as stencils. Spray glues let you place a filmy paper over a richly colored stock for added texture. Glue sticks help you affix the smallest petals and feathers. And flattened sponges can be cut into ivy leaf stamps and used to sponge-print a vine around a package.

The trick is to bring out everything you can think of before you begin, and then let your imagination run. Christmas is always the most special for those who take the time to delve into its riches.

Above: A bit of holiday lace was glued across the bottom of this card. Pressed leaves and grasses were then glued under a satin ribbon bow.

Above: Sponge-stamped stars and leaves, a fern-frond tree, and swirling feathers and ribbons artfully embellish these cards and packages.

Friends Gather to Quilt

By the time our photographer and editor arrived at Sylvia Johnson's house in Marietta, Georgia, the regular Friday quilting group had been stitching little rectangles and squares into houses for about an hour. A table along one wall held plates of cookies and miniature pecan pies, but a large wedge was missing from the coconut cake, and much of the cream cheese-and-pepper-jelly spread was gone. "When we get together, we eat," laughed Alice Berg, one of the group's founding members.

On this sunny December afternoon, the women had gathered to demonstrate a previous year's project for our benefit. The Little Cabin block, was designed by Little Quilts™, a pattern and kit company owned and operated by Alice, Sylvia, and a third member, Mary Ellen Von Holt.

After spending less than an hour with this group, it was easy to imagine what the weekly get-togethers are like. There's a stream of congenial give-and-take: "Look at the color of this sky—see, it's a night sky. I'm into black." "I need a blue door; I want a blue door." "I guess

the grass will be hearts." "What shall I do the roof in?"

And there's a lively flow of conversation that ranges from the comforts of food and quilting books to current events, World War II, Bernina sewing machines, and Eddie Murphy. It's clear that a love of quilting laid the foundation for the group, and bonds of friendship keep it going.

LITTLE CABIN PILLOW

Materials:
patterns and diagram on page 144
plastic template material
fabric scraps: red solid, red check, blue solid, and blue miniprint
⅛ yard of yellow fabric
⅓ yard of green fabric
stuffing
thread to match fabrics

Note: Add ¼″ seam allowance to all pattern pieces.

Make templates from patterns and cut the following: From red solid, cut 2 A's, 1 D, and 1 F. From blue solid, cut 1 E and 2 Cs. From red check, cut 2 A's and 2 Bs. From blue miniprint, cut 1 A and 1 H; reverse pattern and cut 1 H. From yellow, cut 1 A. From green, cut 1 G.

Join pieces following Diagram, being careful to leave seam allowances free. Trim all seams to ⅛″. Press block.

To make borders, from yellow fabric, cut 2 (1¼″ x 5½″) strips and 2 (1¼″ x 7¼″) strips. With right sides facing and raw edges aligned, join a 5½″ strip to each side of quilt block. Join a 7¼″ strip each to top and bottom. From green fabric, cut 2 (2¼″ x 7¼″) strips and 2 (2¼″ x 10½″) strips. Join a 7¼″ strip to each side and a 10½″ strip each to top and bottom. From green fabric, cut a 10½″ square for back. With right sides facing and raw edges aligned, stitch back to quilt block, leaving a 2½″ opening. Turn, stuff pillow, and slipstitch opening closed.

LITTLE CABIN ORNAMENT

Materials (for 1 ornament):
patterns and diagram on page 144
plastic template material
fabric scraps: red, yellow, blue, and green tiny prints and solids
5½″ square of solid fabric for backing
scrap of muslin (optional)
5½″ square of thin quilt batting
thread to match fabrics
6″ (¼″-wide) ribbon

Note: Add ¼″ seam allowance to all pattern pieces.

Make templates as for pillow, but use pattern I for roof and chimneys. Omit sky pieces. Cut 2 Cs and 1 E from 1 fabric scrap. Cut 2 Bs and 2 A's from another fabric scrap. Cut 1 A and 1 D from same fabric scrap or scraps of contrasting colors, as shown in the photo. Cut 1 G from green solid or print for grass. Or cut G from muslin and stitch *Welcome* on it as shown in photo. Join as for pillow, omitting borders.

To assemble ornament, stack batting, backing (right side up), and quilt block (right side down). Stitch, leaving an opening at bottom for turning. Trim excess batting and backing from seams and corners. Clip angles almost to seams at chimneys. Turn right side out and slipstitch opening closed. If desired, quilt in the ditch, along seam lines. For hanger, fold ribbon in half and tack ends to back of roof.

Above: The Little Cabin quilt block can be made into a small pillow (10″ square) or into little ornaments to hang on doorknobs or brighten the Christmas tree.

Knitted Snowflakes and Trees

Whether you choose traditional red and green or colors to match your decor, this knitted tree skirt is sure to become a treasured heirloom. Knit the skirt in one piece and then add a duplicate-stitch pattern of trees and snowflakes reminiscent of Scandinavian ski sweaters.

Materials:
charts and color key on page 147
knitting worsted: 720 yards red, 540 yards white, 180 yards green
size 8 circular (36"-long) knitting needle (or size to obtain gauge)
stitch markers
tapestry needle

Finished Size: Approximately 46" in diameter.
Gauge: 4½ sts and 6 rows = 1" in St st.
Note: When changing colors, remember to wrap old yarn over new so that no holes occur.
Tree Skirt: With red, cast on 534 sts. *Rows 1-8:* Work even in garter st (k every row). Cut yarn. *Row 9:* Join white, p across row. *Row 10:* K across row. *Rows 11-16:* Work in St st according to leaf chart. *Rows 17-25:* Work even in St st with white. *Row 26:* K 29, * ssk, k 15, k 2 tog, k 57, rep from * 6 times more, end last rep with k 30 (520 sts rem). *Row 27 and following odd-numbered rows:* P across row. *Row 28:* K 29, * ssk, k 13, k 2 tog, k 57, rep from * 6 times more, end last rep with k 30 (506 sts rem). *Row 30:* K 29, * ssk, k 11, k 2 tog, k 57, rep from * 6 times more, end last rep with k 30 (492 sts rem). *Row 32:* K 29, * ssk, k 9, k 2 tog, k 57, rep from * 6 times more, end last rep with k 30 (478 sts rem). *Row 34:* K 29, * ssk, k 7, k 2 tog, k 57, rep from * 6 times more, end last rep with k 30 (464 sts rem). *Row 36:* K 29, * ssk, k 5, k 2 tog, k 57, rep from * 6 times more, end last rep with k 30 (450 sts rem). *Row 38:* K 29, * ssk, k 3, k 2 tog, k 57, rep from * 6 times more, end last rep with k 30 (436 sts rem). *Row 40:* K 29, * ssk, k 1, k 2 tog, k 57, rep from * 6 times

more, end last rep with k 30 (422 sts rem). *Row 42:* K 29, * sl 1, k 2 tog, psso, k 57, rep from * 6 times more, end last rep with k 30 (408 sts rem). *Row 44:* K across row. *Rows 45-50:* Work in St st according to leaf chart. *Rows 51 and 52:* Work even in St st with white. Cut yarn. *Rows 53-55:* Join red and work even in garter st. *Row 56:* K 27, * k 2 tog, k 1, place marker on needle, ssk, k 53, rep from * 6 times more, end last rep with k 28 (394 sts rem). *Row 57:* P across row. *Row 58:* K 26, * k 2 tog, k 1, slip marker, ssk, k 51, rep from * 6 times more, end last rep with k 27 (380 sts rem). *Row 59 and following odd-numbered rows:* P across row. *Row 60 and following even-numbered rows:* Continue as established in row 58, decreasing 1 st before and after each marker and having 14 sts fewer at the end of each k row (72 sts rem after row 102). *Rows 103-110:* Work even in garter st. Bind off loosely.

Finishing: With red, pick up sts along side edge of opening and work even in garter st for 8 rows. Bind off loosely. Rep for other side edge. Block gently.

With green, duplicate-stitch trees according to chart (see photograph for placement). (The duplicate-stitch at the end of each branch is worked over a decrease.) With red, duplicate-stitch snowflake pattern between trees according to chart. Work half of snowflake pattern on either side of opening.

Standard Knitting Abbreviations
st(s)—stitch(es)
St st—stockinette stitch (k 1 row, p 1 row)
k—knit
p—purl
ssk—slip, slip, knit
tog—together
rep—repeat
rem—remain
sl—slip
psso—pass slipped stitch over

Diamonds and Bands: Rich Fabric For a Tree Skirt

The diamond shapes and the contrast of light and dark fabrics used in this tree skirt suggest the facets of an exotic gem. If desired, echo the lines and shapes with quilting to further enhance the effect.

Materials:
patterns and diagram on page 154
Note: All fabrics are 45″ wide.
1½ yards light red print fabric
1½ yards dark red print fabric
1 yard cream pindot fabric
16 (2½″ x 16″) strips of red-and-green fabric
thread to match fabrics
3½ yards fabric for backing
3½ yards (45″-wide) thin quilt batting
2 yards (¼″-wide) red satin ribbon

Note: Add ¼″ seam allowance to pattern pieces. All seams are ¼″. Press seams toward darker fabric. If using a patterned stripe, like the one shown, for strips, make sure pattern area is 2″ wide and allows ¼″ on each side for seams.

Enlarge pattern. Transfer pattern A to light red print and cut 8. Reverse pattern, transfer to dark red print, and cut 8.

Enlarge pattern. Transfer pattern B to cream pindot and cut 8. Reverse pattern, transfer to cream pindot, and cut 8.

With right sides facing and raw edges aligned, stitch A to B as indicated on pattern pieces. Repeat for remaining A and B pieces. Stitch A(reverse) to B(reverse) in same manner. Repeat for remaining A(rev) and B(rev) pieces. Press seams.

With right sides facing and raw edges aligned, stitch a strip to the left edge of an A/B unit. Stitch an A(rev)/B(rev) unit to the left edge of the strip, and a strip to the left edge of A(rev)/B(rev) unit. (See Diagram.) Continue alternating pieced units and strips as established to make a circle. Do not join the final strip to first A/B unit. (This will leave an opening to fit around tree.) Trim edges of inner circle in a slight curve. Press seams.

From backing fabric, cut 2 (60″) lengths. With right sides facing and raw edges aligned, stitch along 1 long edge. Open fabric and press seam open. Using skirt top as a pattern and aligning skirt opening with backing seam, trace around top. Cut out backing. Remove stitching along 1 seam of backing to make opening. Press seam. Repeat procedure to piece and cut batting to match. With raw edges aligned, stack batting, skirt top (right side up), and backing (right side down).

To make ties, cut ribbon into 4 (18″) lengths. Pin a length of ribbon to top and bottom of each straight edge of opening, sandwiching ribbon between skirt top and backing. Leaving a 6″ opening for turning along 1 straight edge, stitch around all edges through all layers, catching 1 end of ribbon ties in seam. Trim batting from seam. Clip curves and trim corners. Turn. Turn under raw edges and slipstitch opening closed. Press.

Topstitch ¼″ from edge along opening and around inner circle. Knot ends of ribbon ties.

A Stocking Inspired By the Carousel

A spirited carousel horse with flying mane and tail embellishes this stocking. The bright colors herald the excitement of Christmas, while the cheery verse spreads yuletide joy. And this stocking will hold a myriad of treats.

Materials:
chart, color key, and pattern on page 152
18″ x 23″ (14-count) piece of white Aida cloth
embroidery floss (see color key)
½ yard (36″-wide) white fabric for lining
15″ x 20″ piece of white velvet for back
2 yards of green piping
thread to match

Center design on Aida cloth and work according to chart, using 2 strands of floss, except for areas marked *gold*. For gold areas, use 1 strand of yellow floss with 2 strands of Balger gold blending filament. Backstitch lowercase letters with 2 strands of green and horse with 1 strand of black.

Note: Add ¼″ seam allowance to pattern. All seams are ¼″.

Enlarge pattern; transfer and cut 2 from lining fabric. Center pattern over cross-stitch and cut out for front. Reverse and cut back from velvet.

To make hanger, cut a 5″ piece of piping. Remove stitching and cord; press flat. Fold under ¼″ on long edges. With wrong sides facing, fold in half lengthwise and slipstitch long edges together.

Sew lining pieces with right sides facing, leaving top open. Do not turn. With right sides facing and raw edges aligned, pin piping around side and bottom edges of front and stitch. With right sides facing, pin back to front; stitch on stitching line of piping, leaving top open. Turn and press.

Turn under ¼″ around top of stocking. With raw edges aligned and piping up, pin piping to turned-under edge of stocking. Fold hanger in half to make a loop and, with loop pointed up, baste to inside back of stocking. Slip lining in stocking, turn under ¼″ along top edge, and topstitch around top edge through all layers.

Start Something Cooking

Spend a memorable afternoon baking Christmas cookies with your favorite elf. Our jolly snowman apron is just the right accessory for little kitchen helpers. And with the amount of time spent in the kitchen during the yule season, the festive and functional green quilted apron will surely come in handy.

What better way to present a gift of the goodies the two of you whip up than in a brightly stenciled tin? Old metal tins take on new life with these decorative stencils. With a little adaptation, these designs could be used on square tins or even a metal serving tray. Use your creativity and a copy machine to rearrange the motifs to fit your surface; then finish your gifts with patterned tissue, ribbons, and your home-baked treats.

GREEN QUILTED APRON

Materials:
diagram on page 147
33″ x 39″ piece of green quilted fabric
7¾ yards (½″-wide) red double-fold bias
  tape
thread to match
38″ (1″-wide) white eyelet ruffle

Referring to Diagram, cut apron and pocket from fabric. Machine-stitch ¼″ from the edge all around both pieces to secure quilting threads. Mark bias tape trim placement lines on pocket as shown in Diagram. Cut 2 (10″) lengths of bias tape. Baste folded bias tape in place on placement lines on pocket. Cut 1 (27″) length of bias tape and bind 1 long edge of pocket. Cut 1 (27″) length of eyelet. With eyelet pointing up, stitch bound edge of eyelet to wrong side of bound pocket edge, stitching close to top edge (see photograph).

With raw edges aligned, pin wrong side of pocket to right side of apron front. Using ¼″ seam, stitch through both layers around side and bottom edges of pocket. Topstitch close to both edges of vertical bias tape trim on pocket, stitching through all layers to make 3 pockets.

Cut 1 (9″) length of eyelet. With raw edges aligned and eyelet pointing down, baste bound edge of eyelet to top of apron front. Cut 1 (9″) length of bias tape and bind top edge of apron. Cut 1 (73″) length of bias tape and bind down side edge from waist, across bottom edge, and up to waist on opposite side, mitering corners. Cut 2 (15″) lengths of bias tape. Bind each diagonal edge of apron, extending tape past corners about ½″ on each end. Turn under excess tape and slipstitch to wrong side of apron.

To make waist ties, cut 2 (30″) lengths of bias tape. With bias tape folded, stitch long edges together. Fold under ¼″ on 1 end of each piece of bias tape and stitch to apron at points indicated on Diagram. To make neck ties, cut 2 (24″) lengths of bias tape and finish as for waist ties. Stitch to apron at points indicated on Diagram. Knot ends of all ties.

Right: Christmas baking fills the house with the aromas of the season. Get into the spirit with our festive aprons and then fill stenciled tins with the fruits of your labors.

Make snowman pattern and transfer to white fabric, Christmas print, and batting, and cut 1 of each. Fuse interfacing to 8″ square of red pindot, transfer cheek pattern to interfacing, and cut 2. Fuse interfacing to orange pindot, transfer nose pattern to interfacing, and cut 1. Transfer mitten pattern to quilted red pindot and cut out. Reverse pattern and cut another mitten. From green print, cut 2 (2″ x 28″) strips for waist ties.

For neck strap, with right sides facing, fold red print strip in half lengthwise and stitch along long edge. Turn and press. For waist ties, with right sides facing, fold 1 green print strip in half lengthwise and stitch along long edge and 1 end. Turn and press. Repeat for other waist tie.

Stack snowman pieces in the following order: batting, white cotton for apron front (right side up), and Christmas print for apron back (right side down). Stitch around apron, leaving open where indicated on pattern. Clip curves and angles. Trim batting from seam. Turn and press. Slipstitch opening closed. Tack ends of neck strap to back of apron where indicated on pattern. Tack an end of each waist tie to back of apron where indicated on pattern. To form loop in waist tie, measure 3″ from apron along tie and fold to make a 1½″ loop. Tack loop to apron back at seam. Repeat for other waist tie.

Cut 2 (1½″ x 5″) strips from green print for mitten cuffs. Fold both long edges of 1 cuff under ¼″ and press. With wrong sides facing, fold cuff in half lengthwise and press. Bind edge of mitten with cuff. Repeat for other cuff.

Following Diagram, machine-appliqué mittens, cheeks, and nose with satin stitch and matching thread on apron front. Sew on buttons for eyes (see Diagram). Machine-stitch eyebrows and mouth with satin stitch and red thread as indicated on Diagram.

To make bow tie, with right sides facing, fold ends of red checked fabric together. Stitch around all edges, leaving an opening for turning. Turn, press, and slipstitch opening closed. Hand-pleat tie and tack in center to hold pleats in place. Tack tie to apron (see photograph).

SNOWMAN APRON

Materials:
patterns and diagram on page 148
16″ x 18″ piece of white cotton fabric
16″ x 18″ piece of Christmas print fabric
16″ x 18″ piece of batting
12″ square of fusible interfacing
8″ square of red pindot fabric
2″ x 3″ piece of orange pindot fabric
6″ x 12″ piece of quilted red pindot fabric
7″ x 28″ strip of green print fabric
3½″ x 23½″ strip of red print fabric
2 (1″) flat, black buttons
4½″ x 8½″ piece of red checked fabric
thread to match fabrics

STENCILED GIFT TINS

Materials (for 3 tins):
patterns on page 150
metal tins: 10″ diameter, 7″ diameter, 5″
    diameter
fine-grade steel wool
metal primer rustproof spray paint
flat white and red rustproof spray paint
    (for metal)
.003-gauge mylar (frosted on 1 side)
craft knife
stencil brushes
fine-tip artists' brush
acrylic paints: red, green, peach, light
    brown, gold, black
clear acrylic spray

Sand the outside of each lid and tin with steel wool to remove rust and roughen old paint. Wash in hot soapy water; rinse and dry. Place in a warm oven for several minutes to dry thoroughly.

Spray tins with primer and allow to dry for 24 hours.

Spray outside of lids and large and small tins with 2 or 3 light coats of flat white paint; allow to dry overnight between coats. Spray outside of medium tin red and lid white.

Trace stencil pattern on frosted side of mylar. Make a separate stencil for each paint color. Cut stencils on the shiny side of the mylar. (Errors in cutting can be corrected with small pieces of transparent tape.)

For large tin lid, stencil border stems and leaves green; let dry; then stencil border tulips red. Center angel on lid, using the center markings indicated on pattern. Stencil in this order—Stencil 1: dress, shoes, ribbon, tulips, and trim on dress with red; Stencil 2: face, hands, legs, and wings with peach; Stencil 3: leaves and stems with green; Stencil 4: hair with light brown; Stencil 5: halo with gold; Stencil 6: wing highlights with red. Referring to photo, use fine-tip brush to paint eyes and mouth with black.

For medium tin lid, first stencil border as for large tin. Center scallop design within border and stencil with red. Center tulips and ribbon design within scallop design and stencil with red. Stencil stems and leaves with green.

For small tin lid, first stencil border as above with red. Center ribbon and tulips and stencil with red. Stencil stems and leaves with green. Stencil side of tin in this order: leaves and stems with green, then flowers with red.

Allow paints to dry thoroughly. Spray with clear acrylic.

Above: The bright Christmas prints used for the hearts, birds, and trees stand out dramatically against a white polished cotton background in this holiday table set.

Set the Table With Style

Appliqué hearts, trees, and birds in red and green prints on a white polished cotton field to deck the table with style. A set of place mats, chair backs, and matching table runner would be an ideal gift for new homeowners.

PLACE MAT

Materials (for 1 place mat):
pattern on page 142
scrap of red cotton print for hearts
17¾" x 12¼" piece of white polished
   cotton
½ yard (45"-wide) green cotton
thread to match fabrics
19¾" x 14¼" piece of thin quilt batting
white quilting thread

Note: All seams are ¼" unless otherwise noted.

Transfer place mat heart pattern to red print 3 times and cut out. Clip curves and angles. Using photograph as a guide and turning edges under ⅛", appliqué pieces to white fabric with matching thread.

From green, cut 2 (1½" x 17¾") border strips and 2 (1½" x 14¾") border strips. With right sides facing and raw edges aligned, stitch a 17¾" strip to each long edge of appliquéd piece. Stitch a 14¼" strip to each short edge of appliquéd piece in same manner. Press seams toward green fabric.

From green, cut a 19¾" x 14¼" piece for backing. Stack batting, backing (right side up), and top (right side down). Stitch around edges, leaving an opening for turning. Trim batting from seam. Clip corners and turn. Slipstitch opening closed.

Outline-quilt around each heart and inside green border with white thread. With white thread, quilt parallel diagonal lines, about 1" apart, across white fabric.

TABLE RUNNER

Materials:
patterns and diagram on page 142
scrap of red cotton print #1 for hearts
scrap of red cotton print #2 for birds
scrap of green cotton print #1 for wings
1 yard (45"-wide) green cotton print #2
   for trees and backing
20¼" x 34" piece of white polished
   cotton
⅓ yard (45"-wide) green cotton
thread to match fabrics
24¾" x 38½" piece of thin quilt batting
white and green quilting thread

Note: All seams are ¼" unless otherwise noted.

Transfer table runner heart pattern 4 times to red print #1 and cut out. Transfer bird pattern 6 times to red print #2 and cut out. Transfer wing pattern 6 times to green print #1 and cut out. Transfer tree pattern 8 times to green print #2 and cut out. Clip curves and angles. Referring to Diagram for placement and turning edges under ⅛", appliqué pieces to white fabric with matching thread.

From green, cut 2 (2¾" x 34") border strips and 2 (2¾" x 24¾") border strips. With right sides facing and raw edges aligned, stitch a 34" strip to each long edge of appliquéd piece. Stitch a 24¾" strip to each short edge of appliquéd piece in same manner. Press seams toward green fabric.

From green print #2, cut a 24¾" x 38½" piece for backing. Stack batting, backing (right side up), and top (right side down). Stitch around edges, leaving an opening for turning. Trim batting from seam. Clip corners and turn. Slipstitch opening closed.

Outline-quilt around appliquéd pieces and inside green border with white thread. With white thread, quilt parallel diagonal lines, about 1½" apart, across white fabric. With green thread, quilt a line ¼" from outer edge and a line ¼" from inner edge of border.

Above: These appliqué motifs will lend a country air to any kitchen or dining room. Consider using pretty pastel prints or bright primary solids for a table set that will carry you through the rest of the year.

CHAIR BACK

Materials (for 1 chair back):
patterns on page 142
scrap of red cotton print #1 for hearts
scrap of red cotton print #2 for birds
scrap of green cotton print #1 for wings
scrap of green cotton print #2 for trees
12¼″ square of white polished cotton
½ yard (45″-wide) green cotton
thread to match fabrics
14¼″ square of thin quilt batting
white quilting thread

Note: All seams are ¼″ unless otherwise noted.

Transfer chair back heart pattern 3 times to red print #1 and cut out. With right sides facing, fold red print #2 in half. Transfer bird pattern to folded fabric and cut out. With right sides facing, fold green print #1 in half. Transfer wing pattern to folded fabric and cut out. Transfer tree pattern 3 times to green print #2 and cut out. Clip curves and angles. Using photograph as a guide and turning edges under ⅛″, appliqué pieces to white fabric with matching thread.

From green, cut 2 (1¼″ x 12¼″) border strips and 2 (1¼″ x 14¼″) border strips. With right sides facing and raw edges aligned, stitch a 12¼″ strip to each side edge of appliquéd piece. Stitch a 14¼″ strip to top and bottom edges of appliquéd piece in same manner. Press seams toward green fabric.

To make ties, from green, cut 2 (1¼″ x 45″) strips. With wrong sides facing, fold long edges of 1 strip to meet in center and press. Fold strip in half lengthwise and press. Stitch along long edge with ⅛″ seam. Cut strip in half. Repeat with other green strip. Fold ties in half and tack folds to corners on right side of chair back.

From green, cut a 14¼″ square for backing. Stack batting, backing (right side up), and top (right side down). Stitch around edges, catching folds of ties in seam and leaving an opening for turning. Trim batting from seam. Clip corners and turn. Slipstitch opening closed.

Outline-quilt around appliquéd pieces and inside green border with white thread.

Celebrations from the Kitchen

Food is an integral part of almost every Southern celebration, and at Christmastime tasty treats abound. From breakfast breads that start the day to glorious desserts that end a meal, the foods of the season offer many ways to show off your skill in the kitchen. You are invited to explore international culinary customs and to host a party for Santa and the kids. So whether it's an elegant meal for friends or a delicious gift for everyone on your list, these recipes will fill your holidays with edible delights.

The lunch menu for the Santa Claus party includes Simple Fruit Punch, Santa's Boot Cookies, Party Peanut Butter Sandwiches, Fruit-and-Cheese Kabobs, and Cracker Snack Mix.

100

Goodies for Santa and the Kids

"Santa's coming here—to our house?" Imagine the excitement generated by a personal visit from Santa Claus. Your children will be on their best behavior in anticipation of their guest of honor. With special theme foods like personalized Santa's Boot Cookies and candy cane-shaped Party Peanut Butter Sandwiches, the party is sure to be a success.

Accompany the sandwiches with easy-to-prepare items like Fruit-and-Cheese Kabobs and Cracker Snack Mix. To help pass the time before the great man arrives, organize a Santa Claus Cupcake workshop in your kitchen. Flaked coconut, red cinnamon candies, and chocolate morsels provide the little elves with all they need to make an original take-home treat. And with a little restraint, they'll still have treats to leave out for Santa's Christmas Eve tea.

PARTY PEANUT BUTTER SANDWICHES

- ½ cup peanut butter
- ¼ cup applesauce
- 2 teaspoons honey
- ⅛ teaspoon ground nutmeg
- 12 slices cinnamon-raisin bread
- 12 slices thin-sliced sandwich bread
  Cherry-flavored chewy rolled fruit snack

Combine first 4 ingredients; set aside.

Cut out 24 circles of cinnamon-raisin bread with a 2-inch round cutter; cut out a ¾-inch circle from center of 12 circles, discarding centers. Spread about 1½ teaspoons peanut butter mixture on solid round; top with round cutout.

Cut sandwich bread into 24 candy canes or other desired Christmas shapes. Spread about 1 teaspoon filling on one side of each of 12 candy canes; set aside. Unroll fruit snack; slice into thin strips. Wrap strips candy-cane fashion around remaining 12 candy canes; place on top of filling. Yield: 2 dozen.

CRACKER SNACK MIX

2 cups small pretzels
2 cups goldfish-shaped crackers
1 cup bite-size Cheddar cheese crackers
1 cup crispy rice cereal squares
3 tablespoons butter or margarine, melted
2 teaspoons Worcestershire sauce
½ teaspoon seasoning salt

Combine first 4 ingredients in a large bowl. Combine butter, Worcestershire sauce, and seasoning salt; pour over mixture, tossing to coat.

Spread mixture in a 15- x 10- x 1-inch jellyroll pan. Bake at 250° for 30 minutes, stirring twice. Let cool, and store in an airtight container. Yield: 6 cups.

FRUIT-AND-CHEESE KABOBS

1 (8-ounce) can unsweetened pineapple chunks
1 large apple, cut into ¾-inch pieces
12 whole fresh strawberries
12 seedless grapes
12 (¾-inch) cubes Cheddar cheese
12 (6-inch) thin plastic drinking straws

Drain pineapple, reserving juice. Combine juice and apple, tossing to coat. Arrange fruit and cheese onto straws. Yield: 12 servings.

SIMPLE FRUIT PUNCH

1 (5.5-ounce) package lemonade-flavored drink mix
1 (48-ounce) can unsweetened pineapple juice, chilled
1 (33.8-ounce) bottle ginger ale, chilled
Liquid red food coloring (optional)

Prepare drink mix according to package directions; chill.

Just before serving, stir in juice and ginger ale; add a few drops of food coloring, if desired. Yield: 4½ quarts.

SANTA'S BOOT COOKIES

1 (20-ounce) package refrigerated ready-to-slice sugar cookie dough
2 cups sifted powdered sugar
2 tablespoons lemon juice
2 tablespoons water
Red paste food coloring
Decorator Frosting

Divide dough in half; store 1 portion in refrigerator. Roll dough to ¼-inch thickness on floured wax paper placed on a cookie sheet; cut dough with a 2½- to 3-inch boot-shaped cookie cutter, and freeze dough 10 minutes. Remove from freezer, and transfer dough shapes to ungreased cookie sheets. Bake according to package directions. Cool on wire racks. Repeat procedure with remaining dough.

Combine powdered sugar, lemon juice, and water. Tint about two-thirds of glaze with red food coloring. Using a small art brush, paint top of boot with white glaze and bottom of boot with red glaze.

Spoon Decorator Frosting into a decorating bag fitted with metal tip No. 2; pipe an outline on cookies, and pipe names on cookies using Decorator Frosting. Yield: 2½ dozen.

Decorator Frosting:

1½ tablespoons butter or margarine, softened
1 cup sifted powdered sugar
1 tablespoon milk
¼ teaspoon vanilla extract

Cream butter; add sugar and milk alternately, beating until mixture is a good spreading consistency; stir in vanilla. Yield: ½ cup.

Above: Cupcakes baked in "cake cup" ice cream cones provide a stable base for these decorated goodies. With flaked coconut, chocolate morsels, red cinnamon candies, and a little creativity, children can make an edible portrait of Santa Claus.

SANTA CLAUS CUPCAKES

  1 (18.5-ounce) package white cake mix
    with pudding
26 flat-bottomed "cake cup" ice cream
    cones
  1 (16-ounce) can commercial cream
    cheese frosting
    Flaked coconut, chocolate morsels,
      miniature marshmallows, red
      cinnamon candies

Prepare cake mix according to package directions. Spoon ¼ cup batter into each cone, and place cones in muffin pans. Bake at 350° for 20 to 25 minutes or until a wooden pick inserted in center comes out clean. Cool on wire racks.

Spread about 1 tablespoon frosting on top of each cupcake, and decorate as desired with remaining ingredients. (Do not store in airtight container, as this makes cones soften.) Yield: 26 cupcakes.

Around the World, Around the South

Food and feasting are an essential part of Christmas celebrations all over the world. In the South, weeks of candy making and cake baking build delicious anticipation for the holidays. And our heritage is enriched by customs from other lands, introduced by the ethnic groups that have made the South their home. Here is a taste-tempting sampling of Christmas recipes from the Old World and the New.

Christmas dessert in Italy invariably includes **panettone,** *a raised yeast cake filled with raisins and candied fruit. Originally a Milanese specialty, the dome-shaped cake was part of a Christmas ceremony: The head of the family would cut three large slices, and every member had to eat a little of each piece to ensure prosperity in the coming year.*

PANETTONE

  2 **packages dry yeast**
  1 **cup warm water (105° to 115°)**
  5 **to 5½ cups all-purpose flour, divided**
  ½ **cup butter or margarine, softened**
  ½ **cup sugar**
  3 **eggs**
  1 **teaspoon ground nutmeg**
  ½ **teaspoon salt**
  ½ **cup chopped mixed candied fruit**
  ½ **cup raisins**
  1 **tablespoon butter or margarine,**
      melted
      Honey (optional)

Opposite: On Christmas morning, treat your family to a slice of international tradition. Sweet breads, clockwise from front, are Rosca de Reyes, Lussekatter, *and* Panettone.

Cut a piece of aluminum foil long enough to fit around an 8-inch cakepan, allowing a 1-inch overlap; fold lengthwise into thirds. Lightly brush one side of foil with oil; wrap around outside of cakepan, oiled side against pan. Allow foil to extend 3 inches above rim of cakepan, forming a collar. Secure foil in place with freezer tape; set aside.

Dissolve yeast in warm water in a large mixing bowl; let stand 5 minutes. Add 2 cups flour, ½ cup butter, sugar, eggs, nutmeg, and salt; beat at medium speed of an electric mixer until smooth. Stir in candied fruit, raisins, and enough of the remaining flour to make a soft dough.

Turn dough out onto a floured surface; knead until smooth (about 5 minutes). Place dough in a well-greased bowl, turning to grease top. Cover and let rise in a warm place (85°), free from drafts, 1 hour or until doubled in bulk. (Or, to let dough rise in the microwave, set bowl [non-metal] in a larger shallow dish; pour hot water to a depth of 1 inch in bottom dish. Cover dough loosely with wax paper. Microwave at MEDIUM LOW [30% power] 2 minutes; let stand in the microwave 5 minutes. Repeat microwaving and standing 3 times or until the dough is doubled in bulk, giving the dish a quarter-turn after each microwaving period. Carefully turn dough over in bowl if dough's surface appears to be drying out. Remove from oven.)

Punch dough down; turn out onto a floured surface, and knead 1 minute. Roll dough into a smooth ball; place in prepared pan. Brush top of dough with 1 tablespoon melted butter. Gently cut a small *X* about ½ inch deep in top of loaf. Cover and let rise in a warm place, free from drafts, 1 hour.

Uncover dough, and bake at 325° for 50 to 55 minutes or until loaf sounds hollow when tapped. (Shield bread with aluminum foil after 20 minutes of baking to prevent over-browning.) Cool 10 minutes on a wire rack; remove foil and pan. Brush lightly with honey, if desired. Yield: one 8-inch loaf.

In Mexico, gifts are exchanged on January 6, the Epiphany, when the Magi honored the Christ child. The meal that day often includes Rosca de Reyes *(literally, "Ring of Kings"), a fruit-filled loaf with a tiny doll baked inside to represent the infant Jesus. Whoever receives the doll must hold a party on February 2, Candlemas Day, which commemorates Jesus' presentation in the Temple.*

ROSCA DE REYES

  2 packages dry yeast
  ¼ cup warm water (105° to 115°)
  1 cup warm milk (105° to 115°)
4½ to 5 cups all-purpose flour, divided
  ½ cup butter or margarine, softened
  ½ cup sugar
  ½ teaspoon salt
  1 teaspoon grated lemon rind
  1 teaspoon vanilla extract
  3 eggs
  2 cups chopped mixed candied fruit
  1 cup sifted powdered sugar
  1 to 2 tablespoons hot water
  ½ teaspoon vanilla extract
    Diced mixed candied fruit

Dissolve yeast in warm water; let stand 5 minutes. Add milk, 2 cups flour, and next 6 ingredients; beat at medium speed of an electric mixer until smooth. Stir in 2 cups candied fruit and enough remaining flour to make a soft dough.

Turn dough out onto a floured surface; knead until smooth and elastic (about 5 minutes). Place dough in a well-greased bowl, turning to grease top. Cover and let rise in a warm place (85°), free from drafts, 1 hour or until doubled in bulk. (Or, to let dough rise in the microwave, set bowl [non-metal] in a larger shallow dish; pour hot water to a depth of 1 inch in bottom dish. Cover dough loosely with wax paper. Microwave at MEDIUM LOW [30% power] 2 minutes; let stand in microwave 5 minutes. Repeat microwaving and standing 3 times or until dough is doubled in bulk, giving dish a quarter-turn after each microwaving period. Carefully turn dough over in bowl if dough's surface appears to be drying out. Remove from oven.)

Punch dough down; turn out onto a floured surface, and knead 1 minute. Roll dough into a 20-inch rope; place on a greased baking sheet, and bring ends together to form a ring. Invert a lightly greased 10-ounce custard cup or a small (4- to 4½-inch) bowl in center of dough. Pinch ends together to seal. Cover and let rise in a warm place, free from drafts, 20 minutes. Uncover dough, and bake at 375° for 30 to 35 minutes. (Shield bread with aluminum foil after 20 minutes of baking to prevent over-browning.) Cool on a wire rack.

Combine powdered sugar, 1 tablespoon hot water, and vanilla; add enough remaining water to reach desired consistency. Drizzle over bread, and sprinkle with candied fruit. Yield: 1 loaf.

On December 13, Sweden celebrates Lucia Day, honoring a Sicilian Christian martyred in 304 A.D. Her connection to Sweden dates to the Middle Ages, when a peasant had a vision of Lucia in a radiant white gown, wearing a crown of light and bringing food to relieve the starving people.

In the late 19th century, Lucia Day became the family tradition that it is today. The oldest daughter dresses up as the saint (complete with a crown of lighted candles) and wakes her parents with a tray of hot coffee and saffron-flavored buns. The buns are baked in a variety of shapes based on spirals. The most popular is Lussekatter *(Lucia cats), composed of two crossed spirals. The shape combines Christian and pre-Christian emblems, recalling the Nordic symbol of the sun as well as the sign of the cross. Householders used this sign to ward off the devil, who, they believed, often disguised himself as a cat.*

LUSSEKATTER

- 1 cup milk
- ½ cup butter or margarine
- ½ cup sugar
- 1 package dry yeast
- ¼ cup warm water (105° to 115°)
- 4 to 4½ cups all-purpose flour, divided
- ¾ teaspoon salt
- ¼ teaspoon ground saffron
- 1 egg
- 1 egg, beaten
- 24 raisins

Combine first 3 ingredients in a saucepan; heat until sugar dissolves. Cool to 105° to 115°. Dissolve yeast in warm water in a large mixing bowl; let stand 5 minutes. Stir in milk mixture, 2 cups flour, salt, saffron, and 1 egg; beat at medium speed of an electric mixer until blended. Gradually stir in enough remaining flour to make a soft dough.

Turn dough out onto a floured surface; knead until smooth (about 5 minutes). Place in a well-greased bowl, turning to grease top. Cover and let rise in a warm place (85°), free from drafts, 1 hour or until doubled. (Or, to let dough rise in the microwave, set bowl [non-metal] in a larger shallow dish; pour hot water to a depth of 1 inch in bottom dish. Cover loosely with wax paper. Microwave at MEDIUM LOW [30% power] 2 minutes; let stand in microwave for 5 minutes. Repeat microwaving and standing 3 times or until dough is doubled, giving dish a quarter-turn after each microwaving period. Carefully turn dough over in bowl if dough's surface appears to be drying out. Remove from oven.)

Punch dough down; turn out onto a floured surface, and knead 1 minute. Divide dough into 12 pieces. Roll each piece into a 9-inch rope. Place on greased baking sheets; curl ends in opposite directions, forming *S* shapes. Cover and let rise in a warm place, free from drafts, 40 minutes or until doubled in bulk. Brush with beaten egg, and press a raisin gently in center of each curl. Bake at 350° for 20 minutes or until browned. Cool on a wire rack. Yield: 1 dozen.

The Dutch celebrate St. Nicholas Eve on December 5 with a festive meal for family and friends. The meal always concludes with an array of special sweets, including marzipan, speculaas cookies, and letterbankets, edible initials made of flaky puff pastry filled with almond paste.

Gifts are part of the celebration, but are disguised: The father may find something hidden in the roast duck he's carving, for example. So perhaps it's not too surprising that the dessert itself often honors the mother, with a large letterbanket in the shape of an M.

LETTERBANKETS

- 1 (8-ounce) can almond paste, crumbled
- ⅓ cup sugar
- 1 egg
- 1 teaspoon vanilla extract
- 2 (17¼-ounce) packages frozen puff pastry, thawed
- 1 egg, beaten
- 1 tablespoon water

Combine first 4 ingredients in a small mixing bowl. Beat at medium speed of an electric mixer until smooth; cover and chill.

Roll 1 sheet of pastry on a lightly floured surface into a 10- x 8-inch rectangle. Cut pastry into 4 lengthwise strips. Place strips on a lightly greased baking sheet to form the letter *M*. (Letter will be approximately 10 inches tall and 10 inches wide.) Spread half of almond mixture on pastry to within ½ inch from edges. Roll a second sheet of pastry on a lightly floured surface into a 10- x 8-inch rectangle. Cut into 4 lengthwise strips. Place strips over filling, gently pressing edges of pastry to seal. Repeat procedure with remaining pastry and filling.

Combine beaten egg and water; brush over pastry. Bake at 375° for 25 minutes or until browned. Cool on wire racks. Yield: 2 letters (8 servings each).

*The Greeks welcome the New Year with Basi-
lopetta, a round bread honoring St. Basil, the
patron saint of the poor. Baked with a trinket
or coin inside to symbolize the saint's generos-
ity, the bread is sliced according to ritual: The
first piece is set aside for St. Basil, the second
for the poor, the third goes to the oldest member
of the household, and so on down to the youn-
gest child. Whoever gets the prize is assured
good luck in the New Year. If St. Basil wins, a
donation must be given to the church.*

BASILOPETTA

- 1 package dry yeast
- ¼ cup warm water (105° to 115°)
- 1 cup milk (105° to 115°)
- 4 to 4½ cups all-purpose flour, divided
- 2 eggs
- ¼ cup sugar
- ¼ cup butter or margarine, softened
- ¾ teaspoon salt
- ½ teaspoon ground cinnamon
- ½ teaspoon ground nutmeg
- ½ teaspoon anise seeds, crushed
- 1 teaspoon grated orange rind

Dissolve yeast in warm water in a large
mixing bowl; let stand 5 minutes. Add milk, 2
cups flour, and remaining ingredients. Beat at
medium speed of an electric mixer until
smooth. Stir in enough remaining flour to
make a soft dough.

Turn dough out onto a lightly floured surface, and knead until smooth and elastic
(about 5 minutes). Place dough in a well-
greased bowl, turning to grease top. Cover
and let rise in a warm place (85°), free from
drafts, 1 hour or until doubled in bulk. (Or, to
let dough rise in the microwave, set bowl
[non-metal] in a larger shallow dish; pour hot
water to a depth of 1 inch in bottom dish.
Cover dough loosely with wax paper. Microwave at MEDIUM LOW [30% power] 2

minutes; let stand in microwave 5 minutes.
Repeat microwaving and standing 3 times or
until dough is doubled in bulk, giving dish a
quarter-turn after each microwaving period.
Carefully turn dough over in bowl if dough's
surface appears to be drying out. Remove
from oven.)

Punch dough down; turn out onto a floured
surface, and knead 1 minute. Divide dough
into fourths. Shape 1 portion into a ball; roll
to an 8-inch round. Place in a greased 8-inch
round cakepan. Divide 1 portion of dough in
half; roll each half into a thin rope about ½
inch in diameter. Place 1 rope on outside edge
of 8-inch round of dough, gently pressing
down; pinch ends to seal. Cut and shape remaining rope to make numerals of the new
year, and place in center of loaf. Repeat procedure with remaining portions of dough. Cover
and let rise in a warm place, free from drafts,
20 minutes. Uncover and bake at 350° for 25
minutes. Cool on wire racks. Yield: 2 loaves.

*Under Henry VIII, Christmas in England
meant 12 days of feasting. Along with roast
boar, swan, peacock, partridge, and goose, the
menu included plum pudding and Christmas
pie. The spices that flavored the pie were said to
symbolize the gifts of the Magi, and it was
baked in a rectangular dish, representing the
manger.*

*Never one to do anything in a small way,
Henry required quite a large pie: Hauled into
the dining hall on a cart, it was nine feet long,
weighed 165 pounds, and contained eight
kinds of meat, two bushels of flour, and 24
pounds of butter.*

*Under the Puritans, Christmas pies were
condemned as evidence of ungodly extrava-
gance. Cooks continued to bake the pies but in
ordinary round pans. And perhaps to emphasize the thriftiness of the finely chopped ingredients, they called them "minc'd pyes."*

MINCEMEAT PIE

1 (15-ounce) package refrigerated
    piecrusts
1 (28-ounce) jar prepared mincemeat
1 cup chopped pecans
2 tablespoons orange-flavored liqueur
    or orange juice
    Orange Hard Sauce

Line a 9-inch pieplate with one pastry sheet,
following package directions; set aside.

Combine mincemeat, pecans, and liqueur;
spoon into pastry shell.

Cut remaining pastry into strips with a knife
or pastry wheel. Arrange strips in a lattice
design over mincemeat mixture; seal and flute
edges of pastry.

Bake at 425° for 30 minutes or until golden
brown. Serve warm or cold with Orange Hard
Sauce. Yield: one 9-inch pie.

Orange Hard Sauce:

⅔ cup butter or margarine, softened
2 cups sifted powdered sugar
2 tablespoons orange-flavored liqueur
    or orange juice

Combine all ingredients; beat at medium
speed of an electric mixer until smooth. Yield:
1 cup.

Above: Mincemeat pie was a Christmas favorite with the English colonists who settled the South. Serve it with tangy Orange Hard Sauce for the perfect ending to your holiday meal.

Above: In spite of its elegant looks, the Bûche de Noël, or Yule Log, is surprisingly light. It's made with sponge cake, mocha-flavored "bark," and amaretto filling.

110

While the French celebrate with a meal of rich delicacies on Christmas Eve, they save the best dessert for Christmas Day. Bûche de Noël, representing the yule log, is a rolled sponge cake with an almond-flavored filling and buttercream frosting, scored to resemble bark.

BÛCHE DE NOËL

    4 eggs, separated
 ¼ cup sugar
    1 tablespoon vegetable oil
    1 teaspoon almond extract
 ½ cup sugar
 ⅔ cup sifted cake flour
    1 teaspoon baking powder
 ¼ teaspoon salt
    1 to 2 tablespoons powdered sugar
      Amaretto Filling
      Mocha Buttercream Frosting
      Garnishes: chocolate leaves,
         cranberries

Oil bottom and sides of a 15- x 10- x 1-inch jellyroll pan with vegetable oil; line with wax paper, and oil and flour wax paper. Set aside.

Beat egg yolks in a large mixing bowl at high speed of an electric mixer until thick and lemon colored; gradually add ¼ cup sugar, beating constantly. Stir in vegetable oil and almond extract; set aside.

Beat egg whites (at room temperature) until foamy; gradually add ½ cup sugar, beating until stiff but not dry. Fold egg whites into yolks. Combine flour, baking powder, and salt; gradually fold into egg mixture. Spread batter evenly into prepared pan. Bake at 350° for 8 to 10 minutes.

Sift powdered sugar in a 15- x 10-inch rectangle on a cloth towel. When cake is done, immediately loosen from sides of pan, and turn out onto sugared towel. Carefully peel off wax paper. Starting at narrow end, roll cake and towel together, jellyroll fashion; let cake cool completely on a wire rack, seam side down.

Unroll cake, spread with Amaretto Filling, and carefully reroll cake without towel. Place on serving plate, seam side down.

Diagonally cut a 1-inch piece from one end of cake. Position short piece against top center of longer piece to resemble the knot of a tree, placing cut side out. Thinly spread frosting over cake roll. Score frosting with fork tines to resemble bark. Garnish, if desired. Yield: 8 to 10 servings.

Amaretto Filling:

 ½ teaspoon unflavored gelatin
    1 tablespoon cold water
    1 tablespoon sifted powdered sugar
    1 tablespoon cocoa
 ½ cup whipping cream
 1½ teaspoons amaretto

Sprinkle gelatin over cold water in a small saucepan; let stand 1 minute. Cook over low heat, stirring until gelatin dissolves.

Combine powdered sugar and cocoa. Beat whipping cream at low speed of an electric mixer, gradually adding dissolved gelatin. Increase to medium speed, and beat until mixture begins to thicken. Add powdered sugar mixture, and beat at high speed until soft peaks form. Stir in amaretto. Yield: 1 cup.

Mocha Buttercream Frosting:

 ¼ cup butter or margarine, softened
 2½ cups sifted powdered sugar
 2½ tablespoons cocoa
    2 to 3 tablespoons strong coffee
    1 teaspoon vanilla extract

Cream butter at medium speed of an electric mixer; add powdered sugar, cocoa, 2 tablespoons coffee (at room temperature), and vanilla, beating until fluffy. Add enough remaining coffee, if necessary, to make frosting desired spreading consistency. Yield: 1¼ cups.

A New Year's Eve Extravaganza

Celebrate New Year's Eve in style with a formal dinner party. This menu lets you spend more time with your guests and less in the kitchen. The Four-Cheese Pâté, Braided Bread Ring, and Sparkling Fruit Compote can be made ahead of time, and the remaining dishes are simple enough to complete while your guests enjoy the hors d'oeuvres.

The day of the party will be spent pulling together the finishing touches and the decorations. Fill a champagne bucket with calla lilies, white carnations, and magnolia leaves swirled with silver ribbon. Use additional ribbon on the tabletop and as napkin holders. Place votive candles in stemware and add gold ornaments to complete the luxurious display.

Four-Cheese Pâté
Oyster-Artichoke Soup
Green Salad with Tarragon Vinaigrette
*Beef Tenderloin with Champagne-Mustard
Sauce*
Julienne Vegetable Sauté
Sparkling Fruit Compote
Champagne

FOUR-CHEESE PÂTÉ

- 2 (8-ounce) packages cream cheese, softened
- 1 (4½-ounce) package Camembert cheese, softened
- ½ cup crumbled blue cheese, softened
- 1 cup (4 ounces) shredded Swiss cheese, softened
- 1 tablespoon milk
- 1 tablespoon sour cream
  Braided Bread Ring

Combine cream cheese, Camembert cheese (including rind), and next 4 ingredients in a mixing bowl; beat at medium speed of an electric mixer until smooth. Spoon into an airtight container, and chill up to 1 week. To serve, shape into a ball, and place in center of bread ring. Yield: 3½ cups.

Braided Bread Ring:

- ½ (32-ounce) package frozen bread dough, thawed
- 1 tablespoon butter or margarine, melted

Cut loaf in half lengthwise; shape each half into a 24-inch rope. Place ropes side by side on a greased baking sheet. Twist ropes together; shape into a 9-inch circle, pinching ends together to seal.

Invert a lightly greased 10-ounce custard cup or a small (4- to 4½-inch) bowl in center of dough. Cover and let rise in a warm place (85°), free from drafts, 30 minutes or until doubled in bulk. Bake at 350° for 20 to 30 minutes or until golden brown. Brush lightly with melted butter. To serve, thinly slice. Yield: 1 loaf.

OYSTER-ARTICHOKE SOUP

2 (12-ounce) containers fresh Standard oysters
2 bunches shallots, chopped
⅛ teaspoon dried whole thyme
⅛ teaspoon red pepper
6 bay leaves
½ cup butter or margarine, melted
¼ cup all-purpose flour
2 (14½-ounce) cans ready-to-serve chicken broth
1 (14-ounce) can artichoke hearts, drained and cut into eighths
2 teaspoons chopped fresh parsley
1 cup whipping cream

Drain oysters, reserving 1 cup liquid. Cut each oyster into fourths. Set oysters and liquid aside.

Sauté shallots, thyme, red pepper, and bay leaves in butter in a Dutch oven until shallots are tender. Add flour, stirring until smooth. Cook 1 minute, stirring constantly. Gradually stir in broth and reserved oyster liquid; simmer 15 minutes. Remove bay leaves. Add oysters, artichoke hearts, and parsley; simmer 10 minutes. Stir in whipping cream, and cook until thoroughly heated. Yield: 2 quarts.

GREEN SALAD WITH TARRAGON VINAIGRETTE

½ cup vegetable oil
¼ cup tarragon wine vinegar
¼ cup sugar
½ teaspoon salt
¼ teaspoon pepper
¼ teaspoon hot sauce
1 head Boston lettuce, torn into bite-size pieces
1 head curly endive, torn into bite-size pieces
1 small purple onion, sliced
¾ cup coarsely chopped pecans, toasted

Combine first 6 ingredients in a jar. Cover tightly, and shake vigorously. Chill.

Combine lettuce and remaining ingredients in a large bowl. Shake dressing, and pour over salad, tossing to coat greens. Yield: 8 servings.

BEEF TENDERLOIN WITH CHAMPAGNE-MUSTARD SAUCE

½ cup red wine vinegar
¼ cup vegetable oil
½ teaspoon salt
½ teaspoon pepper
½ teaspoon dried whole thyme
1 (5- to 6-pound) beef tenderloin, trimmed
Champagne-Mustard Sauce

Combine first 5 ingredients. Place tenderloin in a large shallow dish; pour marinade over top, and cover tightly. Refrigerate 8 hours, turning occasionally.

Uncover tenderloin; drain and reserve marinade. Place tenderloin on a rack in a roasting pan; insert meat thermometer, making sure it does not touch fat. Bake at 425° for 45 minutes or until thermometer registers 140° (rare), basting occasionally with marinade. (Bake until thermometer registers 150° for medium-rare or 160° for medium.) Slice in ½-inch slices, and drizzle with Champagne-Mustard Sauce. Yield: 8 servings.

Champagne-Mustard Sauce:

1 tablespoon minced shallots
1 tablespoon vegetable oil
½ cup dry champagne
2 tablespoons butter or margarine
2 tablespoons all-purpose flour
1 cup half-and-half
1 tablespoon Dijon mustard
2 tablespoons butter or margarine, softened

Sauté shallots in hot oil until tender; add champagne. Bring to a boil, and boil until mixture is reduced to ¼ cup. Strain liquid, discarding shallots; set aside.

Melt 2 tablespoons butter in a heavy saucepan over low heat; add flour, stirring until smooth. Cook 1 minute, stirring constantly. Gradually add half-and-half; cook over medium heat, stirring constantly, until mixture is thickened and bubbly. Stir in mustard, 2 tablespoons butter, and reduced champagne mixture; cool slightly. Yield: 1⅓ cups.

JULIENNE VEGETABLE SAUTÉ

1 large sweet red pepper
1 large sweet yellow pepper
2 large carrots, scraped and cut into 2- x ¼-inch strips
1 medium onion, chopped
2 cloves garlic, minced
⅓ cup olive oil
2 large zucchini, cut into 2- x ¼-inch strips
2 teaspoons dried whole basil
½ teaspoon salt
½ teaspoon pepper

Seed red and yellow peppers, and cut them into ¼-inch strips. Sauté peppers, carrots, onion, and garlic in hot oil for 5 minutes. Add zucchini strips, and cook for 2 minutes or until vegetables are tender. Stir in basil, salt, and pepper. Yield: 8 servings.

SPARKLING FRUIT COMPOTE

½ cup sugar
1 cup water
Grated rind from 1 lemon
Juice from 1 lemon
4 oranges, peeled and sectioned
2 cups seedless grapes, halved
2 cups cubed fresh pineapple
1 cup sliced strawberries
2 kiwifruit, peeled and sliced
2 cups dry champagne, chilled

Combine sugar and water in a saucepan. Bring to a boil, stirring constantly. Cover, reduce heat, and simmer 5 minutes. Uncover and let cool. Stir in lemon rind and juice.

Combine orange sections, grapes, and pineapple in a large bowl; pour sugar mixture over fruit, tossing to coat. Cover and chill up to 24 hours.

Just before serving, stir in strawberries, kiwifruit, and champagne. Serve in stemmed compotes. Yield: 8 servings.

Above: White Christmas Punch served in glass punch cups is a beautiful addition to any festive occasion. A ribbon tied around the handle of the punch cup adds just the right touch of color.

Beverages

WHITE CHRISTMAS PUNCH

2 cups sugar
1 cup water
1 (12-ounce) can evaporated milk
1 tablespoon almond extract
3 (½-gallon) cartons vanilla ice cream, softened
6 (2-liter) bottles lemon-lime carbonated beverage, chilled

Combine sugar and water in a saucepan. Cook over medium heat until sugar dissolves, stirring constantly. Remove from heat. Add evaporated milk and almond extract; let cool. Chill until ready to serve.

Combine milk mixture and remaining ingredients in punch bowl just before serving, stirring to break ice cream into small pieces. Yield: about 3½ gallons.

RUBY CHRISTMAS SLUSH

2 (6-ounce) cans frozen orange juice concentrate, thawed and undiluted
4½ cups water
2 (46-ounce) cans red fruit punch
1 (46-ounce) can unsweetened pineapple juice
1 (48-ounce) bottle cranapple juice
2 (33.8-ounce) bottles ginger ale, chilled

Combine thawed orange juice concentrate and water, mixing well. Stir in fruit punch, pineapple juice, and cranapple juice. Freeze in a large container, stirring occasionally.

Remove from freezer 3½ hours before serving, stirring occasionally as mixture thaws. Stir in ginger ale just before serving. Yield: about 2¼ gallons.

EASY EGGNOG

½ to ¾ cup light crème de cacao
½ to ¾ cup light rum
½ to ¾ cup brandy
1 quart commercial dairy eggnog
3 pints vanilla ice cream, softened

Combine crème de cacao, rum, brandy, eggnog, and softened vanilla ice cream in a punch bowl, stirring to break ice cream into small pieces. Yield: 9 cups.

MOCHA PUNCH

3 cups water
¼ cup sugar
¼ cup instant coffee granules
⅓ cup chocolate syrup
1 quart milk
½ gallon vanilla ice cream, softened
1 cup Kahlúa (optional)

Combine first 4 ingredients in a small saucepan. Bring to a boil over medium heat; boil 1 minute. Cover and refrigerate at least 8 hours.

When ready to serve, combine coffee mixture, milk, and ice cream in a punch bowl, stirring to blend. Add Kahlúa, if desired. Yield: about 4 quarts.

TIP: When squeezing fresh lemons or oranges for juice, first grate the rind by rubbing washed fruit against surface of grater, taking care to remove only outer colored portion of the rind. Wrap in plastic in teaspoon-size portions and freeze for future use.

ORANGE WASSAIL

1 (64-ounce) carton orange juice
1 (64-ounce) jar apple juice
1 (32-ounce) jar cranberry juice cocktail
1 (12-ounce) can frozen lemonade concentrate, thawed and undiluted
1 (2-inch) stick cinnamon
1 tablespoon whole cloves
2 oranges, sliced

Combine first 5 ingredients in a large kettle. Insert cloves into orange slices, and add to juice mixture. Cook until thoroughly heated. Serve hot. Yield: about 5½ quarts.

MARMALADE TEA

5 cups boiling water
1 family-size tea bag
½ cup orange marmalade
2 tablespoons sugar
2 tablespoons lemon juice

Pour boiling water over tea bag; cover and steep 5 minutes. Remove tea bag, squeezing gently. Stir in marmalade, sugar, and lemon juice. Strain mixture, if desired; serve hot. Yield: 5 cups.

HOT CRANBERRY SIPPER

2 cups cranberry juice cocktail
1 (6-ounce) can unsweetened pineapple juice
½ cup unsweetened orange juice
¼ cup lemon juice
½ cup red currant jelly
¼ teaspoon ground allspice

Combine all ingredients in a large saucepan; cook over medium heat until jelly melts and mixture is thoroughly heated, stirring well. Serve hot. Yield: 1 quart.

Breads

PECAN COFFEE CAKE

    3 cups biscuit mix
    ¼ cup sugar
    ½ cup milk
    ¼ cup butter or margarine, melted
    1 (8-ounce) package cream cheese,
        softened
    ½ cup sugar
    2 eggs
    ½ teaspoon vanilla extract
    ¼ teaspoon butter flavoring
      Brown Sugar Glaze
      Pecan halves

Combine first 4 ingredients in a mixing bowl; stir vigorously until blended. Turn dough out onto a lightly floured surface, and knead 4 or 5 times. Press into bottom and up sides of an ungreased 9-inch round cakepan.

Combine cream cheese, sugar, eggs, vanilla, and butter flavoring in a mixing bowl; beat at medium speed of an electric mixer until smooth. Pour mixture over dough. Bake at 350° for 35 to 40 minutes or until center is set. Cool in pan 15 minutes. Spoon Brown Sugar Glaze over top, and arrange pecan halves over edge of glaze. Serve warm or at room temperature. Yield: 8 servings.

Brown Sugar Glaze:

    2 tablespoons firmly packed brown
        sugar
    2 tablespoons butter or margarine
    1 tablespoon milk

Combine all ingredients in a small saucepan; bring to a boil over medium heat, and cook 2 minutes, stirring constantly. Remove from heat; cool to lukewarm. Yield: about ¼ cup.

GINGERBREAD SCONES

    2¼ cups all-purpose flour
    1 teaspoon baking powder
    ¼ teaspoon baking soda
    1 teaspoon ground cinnamon
    ½ teaspoon ground ginger
    ¼ teaspoon ground allspice
    ¼ teaspoon ground nutmeg
    ½ cup butter or margarine
    ½ cup currants
    ⅓ cup molasses
    ¾ cup whipping cream
      Lemon Butter

Combine first 7 ingredients; cut in butter with a pastry blender until mixture resembles coarse meal. Stir in currants. Add molasses and whipping cream, stirring just until dry ingredients are moistened. Turn dough out onto a lightly floured surface, and knead lightly 4 or 5 times.

Roll dough to ½-inch thickness on a lightly floured surface; cut with a 2-inch biscuit cutter. Place on a lightly greased baking sheet. Bake at 425° for 8 to 10 minutes or until lightly browned. Serve with Lemon Butter. Yield: 2 dozen.

Lemon Butter:

    ¼ cup butter or margarine, softened
    ¼ cup sifted powdered sugar
    1 teaspoon grated lemon rind
    1 tablespoon lemon juice

Combine all ingredients, stirring until blended. Yield: ¼ cup.

Opposite: Start the day in style with hot coffee and a delicately spiced or fruity bread. Pictured here are Pecan Coffee Cake, Holiday Banana-Nut Bread, and Gingerbread Scones with Lemon Butter.

120

FETA CHEESE BREAD

4 to 4½ cups all-purpose flour, divided
2 teaspoons sugar
½ teaspoon salt
1 package rapid-rise yeast
1½ cups milk
¼ cup water
¼ cup shortening
¼ cup butter or margarine, softened
    and divided
4 ounces feta cheese, crumbled and
    divided
2 tablespoons butter or margarine,
    melted

Combine 2 cups flour, sugar, salt, and yeast in a large mixing bowl; stir well. Combine milk, water, and shortening; heat until shortening melts, stirring occasionally. Cool to 125° to 130°.

Gradually add liquid mixture to flour mixture, beating well at medium speed of an electric mixer. Gradually stir in enough remaining flour to make a soft dough.

Turn dough out onto a well-floured surface, and knead 4 or 5 times. Divide dough in half. Roll each half into a 16- x 8-inch rectangle. Spread 2 tablespoons butter over each rectangle; sprinkle each with half of cheese. Roll dough jellyroll fashion, starting at long side; pinch seam to seal. Fold ends under, pinching to seal, and place, seam side down, in greased French bread pans. Brush each with 1 tablespoon melted butter. Cover and let rise in a warm place (85°), free from drafts, about 45 minutes or until doubled in bulk. Bake at 375° for 15 minutes. Reduce temperature to 350°, and bake an additional 20 minutes or until loaves sound hollow when tapped. Remove bread from pans immediately. Yield: 2 loaves.

Opposite: Melted feta cheese permeates these loaves of Feta Cheese Bread. The light texture and flavor of Sweet Potato Crescent Rolls enhance any meal.

SWEET POTATO CRESCENT ROLLS

2 packages dry yeast
1 cup warm water (105° to 115°)
1 cup cooked mashed sweet potato
½ cup shortening
½ cup sugar
1 egg
1½ teaspoons salt
5¼ to 5¾ cups all-purpose flour
¼ cup butter or margarine, softened

Dissolve yeast in warm water in a large mixing bowl; let stand 5 minutes. Add sweet potato, shortening, sugar, egg, and salt; beat at medium speed of an electric mixer until thoroughly blended. Gradually stir in enough flour to make a soft dough.

Turn dough out onto a well-floured surface, and knead until smooth and elastic (about 5 minutes). Place in a well-greased bowl, turning to grease top. Cover and let rise in a warm place (85°), free from drafts, 1 hour or until doubled in bulk. (Or, to let dough rise in the microwave, set bowl [non-metal] in a larger shallow dish; pour hot water to a depth of 1 inch in the bottom dish. Cover dough loosely with wax paper. Microwave at MEDIUM LOW [30% power] 2 minutes; let stand in microwave 5 minutes. Repeat microwaving and standing procedures 3 times or until dough is doubled in bulk, giving the dish a quarter-turn after each microwaving period. Carefully turn dough over in bowl if dough's surface appears to be drying out. Remove from oven.)

Punch dough down, and divide into 3 equal parts. Roll each into a 12-inch circle on a lightly floured surface; spread each circle with 1 tablespoon plus 1 teaspoon butter. Cut each circle into 12 wedges; roll up each wedge, beginning at a wide end. Place on lightly greased baking sheets, point side down, curving slightly to form a crescent.

Cover crescent rolls and let rise in a warm place, free from drafts, 30 to 45 minutes or until rolls are doubled in bulk. Bake at 400° for 10 to 12 minutes or until golden brown. Yield: 3 dozen.

HOLIDAY BANANA-NUT BREAD

1½ cups all-purpose flour
1 teaspoon baking soda
1 cup sugar
2 eggs, beaten
½ cup butter or margarine, melted
1 cup mashed ripe bananas
1 teaspoon vanilla extract
½ cup chopped pecans
¼ cup flaked coconut
¼ cup raisins

Combine first 3 ingredients; set aside.

Combine eggs and next 3 ingredients in a large bowl; add flour mixture, stirring just until moistened. Fold in pecans, coconut, and raisins.

Pour batter into a greased and floured 8½- x 4½- x 3-inch loafpan. Bake at 350° for 1 hour or until a wooden pick inserted in center comes out clean. Cool in pan 10 minutes; remove from pan, and cool completely on a wire rack. Yield: 1 loaf.

APPLE FRENCH TOAST

3 eggs
½ cup milk
½ cup apple juice
1 (8-ounce) carton softened cream cheese
3 tablespoons honey
2 teaspoons grated lemon rind
⅛ teaspoon ground allspice
8 (1½-inch-thick) slices French bread
3 tablespoons butter or margarine, divided
Poached Apple Slices
Caramel Syrup

Combine eggs, milk, and apple juice; beat well. Set aside.

Combine cream cheese, honey, lemon rind, and allspice. Make a horizontal slit in each bread slice, cutting to within ¼-inch of edge; spoon about 1 tablespoon cheese filling into each pocket. Place bread in a 13- x 9- x 2-inch baking dish. Pour egg mixture over bread slices; turn slices to coat evenly. Cover and soak 15 minutes or refrigerate up to 8 hours.

Melt 1½ tablespoons butter in a large skillet; arrange 4 slices bread in skillet, and sauté 4 minutes on each side or until browned. Repeat procedure with remaining butter and bread slices. Serve with Poached Apple Slices and Caramel Syrup. Yield: 4 servings.

Poached Apple Slices:

3 large cooking apples, unpeeled and sliced
1 cup water
2 teaspoons lemon juice

Combine all ingredients in a Dutch oven. Bring to a boil; reduce heat, and simmer 5 minutes or until crisp-tender. Drain. Yield: about 3 cups.

Caramel Syrup:

2 cups sugar
¾ cup boiling water

Sprinkle sugar in a 10-inch heavy cast-iron skillet; cook over medium heat, stirring constantly, until sugar melts and turns a light golden brown. Gradually add boiling water, stirring to make a smooth syrup. Yield: 1½ cups.

Candies and Cookies

CHOCOLATE-ALMOND PRALINES

1½ cups sugar
¾ cup firmly packed brown sugar
½ cup milk
⅓ cup butter
1½ cups slivered almonds, toasted
½ cup semisweet chocolate morsels
1 tablespoon Kahlúa (optional)

Combine sugar, milk, butter, and almonds in a heavy saucepan. Cook over low heat, stirring gently, until sugar dissolves. Cover and cook over medium heat for 2 to 3 minutes to wash down sugar crystals from sides of pan. Uncover and cook mixture to soft ball stage (238°), stirring constantly.

Remove mixture from heat, and stir in chocolate morsels and Kahlúa, if desired. Beat with a wooden spoon just until mixture begins to thicken. Working rapidly, drop mixture by tablespoonfuls onto lightly greased wax paper, and let pralines stand until firm. Yield: 2½ dozen.

Above: Irresistible candies like Chocolate-Covered Cherries, Almond Fudge, and Chocolate-Almond Pralines will quickly disappear. Be sure to save a few for the family.

CHOCOLATE-COVERED CHERRIES

¼ cup butter or margarine, softened
⅔ cup sweetened condensed milk
1 (16-ounce) package powdered sugar, sifted
  Pinch of salt
1 cup flaked coconut
2 (6-ounce) bottles maraschino cherries
12 ounces chocolate-flavored candy coating

Cream butter; add condensed milk, powdered sugar, and salt, beating well. Stir in coconut; cover and chill at least 2 hours.

Drain cherries, and dry thoroughly on paper towels. Shape a small amount of sugar mixture around each cherry. Place on a wax paper-lined baking sheet; chill about 2 hours or until firm.

Place candy coating in top of a double boiler; bring water to a boil. Reduce heat to low; cook until coating melts. Dip each covered cherry into melted coating. Place on wax paper to cool. Store in a cool place. Yield: 4 dozen.

ALMOND FUDGE

2 cups sugar
½ cup sour cream
⅓ cup light corn syrup
2 tablespoons butter or margarine
1 cup chopped almonds, toasted
¼ teaspoon almond extract

Combine first 4 ingredients in a small Dutch oven; bring to a boil. Cover and boil 3 minutes. Uncover and cook, without stirring, until mixture registers 232° on candy thermometer. Remove from heat; let stand 15 minutes.

Add almonds and almond extract; beat with a wooden spoon until fudge thickens (about 5 minutes).

Pour mixture into a buttered 8-inch square pan. Cover and chill; cut into squares. Yield: 1½ pounds.

BRICKLE DESSERT WAFERS

½ cup firmly packed brown sugar
½ cup sugar
⅓ cup vegetable oil
1 egg
½ teaspoon almond extract
1½ cups all-purpose flour
½ teaspoon baking soda
½ teaspoon salt
½ cup almond brickle

Combine first 5 ingredients; beat at medium speed of an electric mixer until blended.

Combine flour, soda, and salt; add to creamed mixture, beating well.

Divide dough into fourths; shape each portion into a 15- x 1½-inch log on a lightly greased cookie sheet, and flatten each log with palm of hand into a 3-inch wide strip. Cut each strip diagonally into 1½-inch slices. Sprinkle with almond brickle. Bake at 375° for 7 to 9 minutes. Cool 2 minutes on cookie sheets; remove to wire racks to cool completely. Yield: 2½ dozen.

ALMOND COOKIES

1 cup butter or margarine, softened
⅔ cup sugar
2 egg yolks
½ teaspoon almond extract
2½ cups all-purpose flour
¼ teaspoon salt
¼ cup sugar
¼ cup ground almonds
2 egg whites, slightly beaten
  Sliced almonds (optional)

Cream butter; gradually add ⅔ cup sugar, beating at medium speed of an electric mixer until light and fluffy. Add egg yolks, one at a time, beating after each addition. Stir in almond extract.

Combine flour and salt; add to creamed mixture, mixing well. Shape dough into a ball; cover and chill at least 2 hours.

Use cookie gun fitted with a flower or pinwheel disc to shape dough, following manufacturer's directions. Place cookies on lightly greased baking sheets. Combine ¼ cup sugar and ground almonds; brush cookies with egg white, and sprinkle with sugar mixture. Place sliced almonds between indentations of flowers, if desired. Bake at 375° for 8 to 10 minutes or until lightly browned. Cool on wire racks. Yield: 4 dozen.

LAYERED BAR COOKIES

½ cup butter or margarine, softened
¼ cup sugar
1 cup all-purpose flour
¼ cup cornstarch
  Pinch of salt
2 eggs, slightly beaten
1 cup firmly packed brown sugar
1 cup chopped pecans
2 tablespoons all-purpose flour
1 teaspoon vanilla extract
1 (7-ounce) can flaked coconut
1 (3-ounce) package cream cheese, softened
¼ cup butter or margarine, softened
1¾ cups sifted powdered sugar
½ teaspoon vanilla extract

Cream ½ cup butter and ¼ cup sugar; gradually add 1 cup flour, cornstarch, and salt, mixing well. Press mixture into a lightly greased 13- x 9- x 2-inch pan. Bake at 350° for 5 to 8 minutes. Remove from oven, and reduce oven temperature to 300°.

Combine eggs and next 5 ingredients, stirring until blended. Spread mixture over crust in pan. Bake at 300° for 15 minutes; increase oven temperature to 350°, and bake an additional 5 to 7 minutes. Cool completely on a wire rack.

Beat cream cheese and ¼ cup butter at high speed of an electric mixer until fluffy; add powdered sugar and ½ teaspoon vanilla, beating until blended. Spread mixture over bar cookies. Cover and chill at least 4 hours. Cut into bars, and store in an airtight container in refrigerator. Yield: 6 dozen.

COCOA SURPRISE COOKIES

1 cup butter or margarine, softened
⅔ cup sugar
1⅔ cups all-purpose flour
¼ cup cocoa
½ teaspoon vanilla extract
½ teaspoon chocolate menthe or mint flavoring
1 cup finely chopped pecans
1 (6-ounce) package crème de menthe wafers, unwrapped
1 cup sifted powdered sugar
1½ tablespoons milk
  Few drops green food coloring

Cream butter; gradually add ⅔ cup sugar, beating until light and fluffy. Add flour and cocoa, mixing well. Stir in flavorings and pecans. Cover and chill dough 2 hours or until firm.

Shape dough into 36 balls. Shape each ball into an oval shape around each crème de menthe wafer. Place on ungreased cookie sheets, and chill 30 minutes. Bake at 375° for 12 minutes. Cool slightly on cookie sheets; remove to wire racks to cool completely.

Combine powdered sugar and milk, stirring until smooth; color with green food coloring. Place mixture in a heavy-duty zip-top plastic bag. Using scissors, snip a tiny hole in a bottom corner of bag; drizzle frosting over cookies. Yield: 3 dozen.

Above: These decorative cookies are as beautiful as they are tasty. Embellish your table with Raspberry Sandwich Cookies, Cocoa Surprise Cookies, and Chocolate-Hazelnut Sticks.

RASPBERRY SANDWICH COOKIES

  1 **cup butter, softened**
  ½ **cup sifted powdered sugar**
2½ **cups all-purpose flour**
  1 **teaspoon vanilla extract**
  ½ **cup raspberry preserves**

Cream butter; gradually add powdered sugar, beating at medium speed of an electric mixer. Add flour and vanilla, mixing well. Shape dough into a ball.

Roll dough to ⅛-inch thickness on a lightly floured surface. Cut with a 2-inch round cutter. Use a ¾-inch cutter to cut out a flower or some other decorative design in center of half the cookies. Pierce solid cookies with the tines of a fork. Place cookies on ungreased cookie sheets. Bake at 300° for 20 minutes or until the cookies are very lightly browned. Cool cookies on wire racks.

Just before serving, spread top of each solid cookie with about ½ teaspoon of raspberry preserves. Top each with cookie cutout. Yield: 3 dozen.

CHOCOLATE-HAZELNUT STICKS

⅔ cup whole hazelnuts or almonds
½ cup butter, softened
⅓ cup sugar
1 egg
¾ teaspoon vanilla extract
1¼ cups all-purpose flour
Chocolate Glaze

Bake hazelnuts on a baking sheet at 325° for 20 minutes, stirring occasionally. Cool 5 minutes; rub between hands to loosen skins; discard skins. Position knife blade in food processor bowl; add hazelnuts, and process until coarsely chopped. Set aside 3 tablespoons nuts for garnish, and finely grind remaining nuts.

Cream butter; gradually add sugar, beating until light and fluffy. Add egg and vanilla, beating until blended. Gradually add flour, beating until smooth. Fold in finely ground hazelnuts.

Use cookie gun fitted with a star-shaped disc to shape dough into decorative 2½-inch sticks, following manufacturer's directions. Place sticks on lightly greased cookie sheets. Bake at 350° for 9 to 11 minutes or until lightly browned. Cool slightly on cookie sheets; remove to wire racks to cool completely. Dip one end of each cookie in Chocolate Glaze, and sprinkle with reserved nuts. Yield: 6 dozen.

Chocolate Glaze:

1 egg white
½ cup sifted powdered sugar
⅓ cup cocoa
⅛ teaspoon ground cinnamon
2 tablespoons butter, softened
2 tablespoons hot water
½ teaspoon vanilla extract

Beat egg white at medium speed of an electric mixer until frothy. Gradually add powdered sugar, cocoa, and cinnamon. Add butter, water, and vanilla, beating until blended. Yield: ⅔ cup.

Note: Cookies can be frozen in an airtight container with wax paper between layers up to 1 month.

BLONDE BROWNIES WITH CHOCOLATE CHUNKS

1 (6-ounce) vanilla-flavored baking bar
⅓ cup butter or margarine
2 eggs, beaten
½ cup sugar
¼ teaspoon vanilla extract
1½ cups all-purpose flour
½ teaspoon baking powder
¼ teaspoon salt
⅔ cup chopped pecans
⅔ cup semisweet chocolate chunks

Combine baking bar and butter in a heavy saucepan; cook over low heat until melted. Set aside to cool slightly.

Combine eggs, sugar, and vanilla in a large bowl, stirring until blended. Add butter mixture, mixing well.

Combine flour, baking powder, and salt; stir into butter mixture. Fold in pecans and chocolate chunks. Spoon into a greased 9-inch square pan. Bake at 350° for 25 minutes. Cool and cut into squares. Yield: 3 dozen.

Festive Desserts

CRANBERRY SHERBET

3 cups fresh cranberries
1 cup sugar
¾ cup water
½ cup orange juice
4 ice cubes
2 tablespoons lemon juice
¾ cup half-and-half

Combine first 4 ingredients in a large saucepan; bring to a boil. Reduce heat, and simmer 6 to 8 minutes or until skins pop. Cool.

Pour mixture into container of an electric blender, and process until smooth. Strain mixture, discarding skins. Return strained mixture to blender. Add ice cubes and remaining ingredients; process until smooth.

Pour mixture into an 8-inch square pan; cover and freeze 2 hours or until slushy. Spoon mixture into a bowl; beat with an electric mixer until fluffy. Repeat procedure. Return mixture to pan; cover and freeze until firm. Yield: 4 cups.

FRENCH CREAM WITH STRAWBERRY SAUCE

1 envelope unflavored gelatin
¼ cup cold water
1 (8-ounce) carton sour cream
1 cup whipping cream
¾ cup sugar
1 (8-ounce) package cream cheese, softened
½ teaspoon almond extract
Strawberry Sauce
Garnishes: star fruit slices, kiwifruit slices

Sprinkle gelatin over cold water in a medium saucepan; let stand 1 minute. Cook over low heat, stirring until gelatin dissolves.

Combine sour cream and whipping cream; beat at medium speed of an electric mixer until blended. Gradually add sugar; beat well. Gradually add gelatin mixture; beat well.

Beat cream cheese at high speed of an electric mixer until light and fluffy; add gelatin mixture and almond extract, beating well. Spoon mixture evenly into seven ½-cup molds; chill until firm.

Unmold on individual plates, and spoon about 1½ tablespoons Strawberry Sauce on one side of plate. Garnish, if desired. Yield: 7 servings.

Strawberry Sauce:

1 (10-ounce) package frozen sliced strawberries, thawed
1 tablespoon cornstarch
2 tablespoons red currant jelly
¼ teaspoon almond extract

Place strawberries in container of an electric blender; process until smooth. Strain strawberries, and discard seeds.

Combine cornstarch and remaining ingredients in a small saucepan, stirring until cornstarch dissolves; stir in strawberry puree. Cook over medium heat, stirring constantly, until mixture comes to a boil. Let boil 1 minute, stirring constantly. Remove from heat. Cover and chill. Yield: ¾ cup.

Opposite: French Cream with Strawberry Sauce is an elegant ending to a holiday dinner. Garnish with kiwifruit and star fruit slices for a touch of seasonal color.

HOLIDAY ICE CREAM BOMBE

8 macaroon cookies, crumbled
⅔ cup chopped red and green candied
    cherries
⅓ cup bourbon
⅔ cup chopped pecans, toasted
½ gallon vanilla ice cream, softened

Line a 2-quart bowl or tall mold smoothly with aluminum foil; set aside.

Combine first 3 ingredients; let stand 30 minutes. Fold in pecans and ice cream. Spoon into prepared bowl. Cover and freeze at least 8 hours.

To unmold and serve, invert bowl onto a serving plate; carefully remove foil. Cut into wedges to serve. Yield: 14 to 16 servings.

FESTIVE FRUIT PIE
WITH CINNAMON SAUCE

    Pastry for double-crust 9-inch pie
3 medium-size cooking apples, peeled
    and sliced
2 medium-size pears, peeled and sliced
1 cup fresh cranberries
1 tablespoon lemon juice
½ cup sugar
½ cup firmly packed brown sugar
¼ cup all-purpose flour
½ teaspoon ground cinnamon
¼ teaspoon ground nutmeg
2 tablespoons butter or margarine
    Cinnamon Sauce

Roll half of pastry to ⅛-inch thickness on a lightly floured surface. Fit into a 9-inch deep-dish pieplate. Set aside.

Combine apples and next 3 ingredients; toss gently. Combine ½ cup sugar and next 4 ingredients; add to apple mixture, and toss gently. Spoon filling into pastry shell, and dot with butter.

Roll out remaining pastry to ⅛-inch thickness on a lightly floured surface, and place over filling. Trim edges; seal and flute. Cut several slits in top crust to allow steam to escape. Bake at 375° for 45 minutes. Serve with Cinnamon Sauce. Yield: one 9-inch pie.

Cinnamon Sauce:

½ cup sugar
2 tablespoons cornstarch
1 cup water
3 tablespoons lemon juice
1 tablespoon butter or margarine
1 teaspoon ground cinnamon
½ teaspoon ground nutmeg

Combine all ingredients in a small saucepan. Cook over medium heat until mixture comes to a boil, stirring constantly. Boil 1 minute, stirring constantly. Serve warm. Yield: 1 cup.

CHOCOLATE-TRUFFLE TORTE

1 cup all-purpose flour
½ cup cocoa
1 teaspoon baking powder
½ teaspoon baking soda
¼ teaspoon salt
8 eggs, separated
1½ cups sugar
2 teaspoons vanilla extract
⅔ cup water
    Truffle Filling
    Whipped Cream Frosting

Grease two 15- x 10- x 1-inch jellyroll pans, and line with wax paper; grease and flour wax paper. Set aside.

Sift first 5 ingredients together; set aside.

Beat egg whites (at room temperature) at high speed of an electric mixer until foamy. Gradually add sugar, beating until soft peaks form. Set aside.

Beat egg yolks until thick and lemon colored; stir in vanilla. Add flour mixture alternately with water, beating at low speed of an electric mixer, beginning and ending with flour mixture.

Fold egg whites into batter. Spread batter evenly into prepared pans. Bake at 375° for 10 to 12 minutes or until a wooden pick inserted in center comes out clean.

When layers are done, immediately loosen from sides of pans, and turn out onto wire racks to cool. Peel off wax paper. When completely cool, cut each cake crosswise into 3 strips of equal length.

Stack cake layers on serving plate, spreading Truffle Filling between layers. Spread Whipped Cream Frosting on top and sides of cake, reserving 1 cup for piping.

Spoon reserved Whipped Cream Frosting into a decorating bag fitted with large fluted tip No. 5 or 6B. Pipe frosting around top border of cake. Chill until serving time. Yield: 12 servings.

Truffle Filling:

1½ cups semisweet chocolate morsels
3 egg yolks
¼ cup plus 2 tablespoons butter or margarine, cut into cubes
¼ cup plus 2 tablespoons sifted powdered sugar
3 tablespoons milk

Place chocolate morsels in top of a double boiler; bring water to a boil. Reduce heat to low; cook until chocolate melts. Remove container of chocolate from over boiling water. Set aside.

Beat egg yolks until thick and lemon colored. Gradually stir about one-fourth hot melted chocolate into yolks; add to remaining hot mixture, stirring constantly. Add butter and powdered sugar; beat at medium speed of an electric mixer until butter melts and mixture is smooth; cool.

Add milk to chocolate mixture; beat at high speed of an electric mixer until mixture is spreading consistency. Yield: 1½ cups.

Whipped Cream Frosting:

1½ cups whipping cream
3 tablespoons cocoa
¼ cup sifted powdered sugar
1 teaspoon vanilla extract

Combine all ingredients in a medium-size mixing bowl; beat at high speed of an electric mixer until firm peaks form. Yield: 3 cups.

COFFEE SOUFFLÉ PARFAITS

3 eggs, separated
1 cup water
1 envelope unflavored gelatin
½ cup sugar
2 tablespoons instant coffee granules
1 teaspoon vanilla extract
2 tablespoons crème de cacao
⅓ cup sugar
1 cup whipping cream, whipped
3 (1.2-ounce) English toffee-flavored candy bars, crushed

Beat egg yolks at medium speed of an electric mixer until thick and lemon colored. Combine yolks and water in a saucepan; sprinkle gelatin over yolk mixture, and let stand 1 minute. Add ½ cup sugar and coffee granules to gelatin mixture; cook over medium heat, stirring constantly until mixture begins to boil. Remove from heat; stir in vanilla and crème de cacao. Cool.

Beat egg whites (at room temperature) until foamy; gradually add ⅓ cup sugar, beating until firm peaks form. Fold egg whites and whipped cream into yolk mixture.

Spoon soufflé mixture into parfait glasses alternately with crushed candy, ending with candy. Cover and chill at least 4 hours. Yield: 8 servings.

Above: Black Walnut Spice Cake has all the traditional flavors and scents of Christmas.

BLACK WALNUT SPICE CAKE

1½ cups boiling water
1 cup chopped black walnuts
½ cup shortening
½ cup butter or margarine, softened
2 cups firmly packed light brown sugar
3 eggs
3 cups all-purpose flour
1 tablespoon baking powder
Dash of salt
½ teaspoon ground cinnamon
½ teaspoon ground nutmeg
½ teaspoon ground cloves
1 cup milk
Buttery Cinnamon Frosting
Additional chopped black walnuts

Pour boiling water over walnuts; let stand 4 or 5 minutes. Drain well.

Cream shortening and butter in a large mixing bowl; gradually add sugar, beating until light and fluffy. Add eggs, one at a time, beating well after each addition.

Combine flour, baking powder, salt, and spices; add to creamed mixture alternately with milk, beginning and ending with flour mixture. Mix after each addition. Fold in reserved walnuts.

Pour batter into 3 greased and floured 9-inch round cakepans. Bake at 350° for 20 to 25 minutes or until a wooden pick inserted in center comes out clean. Cool in pans 10 minutes; remove from pans, and let cool completely on wire racks. Spread Buttery Cinnamon Frosting between layers and on top and sides of cake. Sprinkle chopped walnuts on top. Yield: one 3-layer cake.

Buttery Cinnamon Frosting:

1 cup butter or margarine, softened
7½ cups sifted powdered sugar, divided
1¼ teaspoons ground cinnamon
¼ cup plus 1 tablespoon milk
2½ teaspoons vanilla extract

Cream butter at high speed of an electric mixer. Combine 2 cups powdered sugar and cinnamon; add to butter, and beat until smooth. Add remaining sugar alternately with milk, beating well after each addition. Add vanilla; beat until smooth and creamy. Yield: enough for one 3-layer cake.

PUMPKIN PIE
WITH SPICED CREAM SAUCE

½ (15-ounce) package refrigerated pastry crust
1 (16-ounce) can pumpkin
1 (14-ounce) can sweetened condensed milk
2 eggs, beaten
¼ cup firmly packed brown sugar
1 teaspoon pumpkin pie spice
¼ teaspoon vanilla extract
Spiced Cream Sauce

Fit pastry into a 9-inch pieplate; fold edges under, and flute. Prick bottom and sides of pastry shell generously with a fork. Bake at 450° for 8 minutes; cool.

Combine pumpkin and next 5 ingredients; pour into prepared crust. Bake at 350° for 50 to 55 minutes or until a knife inserted in center comes out clean. Remove from oven; let cool.

Serve with dollop of Spiced Cream Sauce. Yield: one 9-inch pie.

Spiced Cream Sauce:

2 tablespoons brown sugar
¼ teaspoon pumpkin pie spice
½ cup sour cream
¼ cup whipping cream

Sprinkle brown sugar and pumpkin pie spice over sour cream in a small bowl; stir well. Let stand 3 minutes. Fold in whipping cream, 1 tablespoon at a time, until thoroughly blended. Cover and refrigerate. Yield: ¾ cup.

CHOCOLATE RIPPLE CHEESECAKE

1 (8½-ounce) package chocolate wafer
    cookies, crushed
¼ cup sugar
⅓ cup butter or margarine, melted
2 (8-ounce) packages cream cheese,
    softened
½ cup sour cream
3 eggs
1 teaspoon vanilla extract
1 pound white chocolate, melted
1 (8-ounce) package cream cheese
¼ cup sugar
1 egg
¼ teaspoon vanilla extract
2 (1-ounce) squares semisweet
    chocolate, melted
⅓ cup sour cream
Chocolate Glaze

Combine first 3 ingredients; press onto bottom and 2 inches up sides of a 9-inch springform pan. Set aside.

Combine 2 (8-ounce) packages cream cheese and ½ cup sour cream; beat at medium speed of an electric mixer until fluffy. Add 3 eggs, one at a time, beating after each addition. Add 1 teaspoon vanilla and melted white chocolate, stirring just until blended. Spoon half of mixture over chocolate crust. Set other half aside.

Combine 1 (8-ounce) package cream cheese and ¼ cup sugar; beat at medium speed of an electric mixer until fluffy. Add 1 egg and ¼ teaspoon vanilla; blend well. Stir in melted semisweet chocolate and ⅓ cup sour cream. Spoon gently over white chocolate layer.

Carefully spoon remaining white chocolate mixture over chocolate layer. Bake at 300° for 1 hour or until cheesecake is almost set. Turn oven off, and partially open oven door. Leave cake in oven 30 minutes. Remove from oven; run knife around crust to loosen sides.

Cool on a wire rack; cover and chill at least 8 hours.

Remove outer rim of springform pan, and place cheesecake on serving plate. Spread warm Chocolate Glaze over cheesecake. Yield: one 9-inch cheesecake.

Chocolate Glaze:

6 (1-ounce) squares semisweet
    chocolate
¼ cup butter or margarine
¾ cup sifted powdered sugar
2 tablespoons water
1 teaspoon vanilla extract

Combine chocolate and butter in top of a double boiler; cook until melted. Remove from heat; add remaining ingredients, stirring until smooth. Spread over cheesecake while glaze is warm. Yield: 1 cup.

Party Fare

SAUSAGE-DATE BALLS

1 pound bulk pork sausage
2 cups biscuit mix
1 (8-ounce) package pitted dates, chopped
½ cup finely chopped pecans

Combine all ingredients; mix well, and shape into 1-inch balls. Place on lightly greased baking sheets. Bake at 350° for 20 minutes or until lightly browned. Serve warm or at room temperature. Yield: 4½ dozen.

Note: Sausage-Date Balls may be frozen after cooking. Chill thoroughly, and freeze in airtight container. Thaw at room temperature.

SOUTHWESTERN SHRIMP MINI-TACOS

1½ cups water
2 dozen medium shrimp (about ½ pound)
¼ cup olive oil
1 tablespoon lime juice
1 tablespoon dried whole cilantro
1 teaspoon Dijon mustard
¼ teaspoon ground cumin
⅛ teaspoon salt
⅛ teaspoon pepper
1 (3.8-ounce) package mini-taco shells
1 (6-ounce) package frozen guacamole, thawed
Garnish: parsley

Bring water to a boil; add shrimp, and cook 3 to 5 minutes. Drain well; rinse with cold water. Peel and devein shrimp.

Combine olive oil and next 6 ingredients; pour over shrimp; cover and chill 4 hours.

Place taco shells on a baking sheet, and bake at 350° for 5 to 7 minutes or until crisp.

Remove from oven; cool slightly. Spread each taco shell with 1½ teaspoons guacamole. Drain shrimp, and insert one shrimp into each taco shell. Garnish, if desired. Serve immediately. Yield: 2 dozen.

ANTIPASTO SPREAD WITH TOAST ROUNDS

1 (13-ounce) package French baguettes
⅓ cup olive oil
1 (14-ounce) can artichoke hearts, drained and finely chopped
1 (4-ounce) can sliced mushrooms, drained and finely chopped
1 (2-ounce) jar diced pimiento, drained
¾ cup pitted ripe olives, chopped
¼ cup chopped green pepper
¼ cup chopped celery
¾ cup olive oil
¼ cup white wine vinegar
2 tablespoons water
1 clove garlic, crushed
1 tablespoon dried Italian seasoning
¼ teaspoon pepper
⅛ teaspoon salt

Cut bread with a serrated knife into ⅜-inch thick rounds. Lightly brush tops using ⅓ cup olive oil; place on baking sheets, and bake at 400° for 8 to 10 minutes or until crisp and golden brown. Set aside. (Toast rounds can be stored in an airtight container up to 2 weeks.)

Combine artichokes and next 5 ingredients. Combine ¾ cup olive oil and remaining ingredients in a large jar; cover tightly, and shake vigorously. Pour mixture over artichoke mixture; cover and chill up to 1 week. Drain before serving; serve with toast rounds. Yield: about 4 dozen appetizer servings.

Above: Start your celebration off with the delicious tidbits shown here: Antipasto Spread with Toast Rounds, Southwestern Shrimp Mini-Tacos, and Holiday Pastry Swirls.

135

BACON-WRAPPED SCALLOPS

1 cup all-purpose flour
1 teaspoon salt
1 teaspoon white pepper
1 teaspoon garlic powder
1 teaspoon paprika
1 egg, well beaten
1 cup milk
1 cup dry breadcrumbs
16 slices bacon, partially cooked
32 sea scallops (about 1 pound), drained
Commercial cocktail sauce (optional)

Combine first 5 ingredients in a large shallow dish; stir well, and set aside.

Combine egg and milk in a small bowl; mix well, and set aside. Place breadcrumbs in a shallow dish; set aside. Cut bacon slices in half.

Dredge scallops in flour mixture; shake off excess. Dip scallops into egg mixture, and roll in breadcrumbs. Wrap each scallop with ½ slice bacon, and secure with a wooden pick. Broil 2 minutes; turn scallops, and broil 2 minutes or until done. Serve hot with cocktail sauce, if desired. Yield: 32 scallop appetizers.

CRUNCHY POTATO BITES

1 cup cooked mashed potatoes
1 cup ground cooked ham
½ cup (2 ounces) shredded Swiss cheese
2 tablespoons chopped green onions
1 egg, beaten
3 tablespoons mayonnaise or salad dressing
1 teaspoon prepared mustard
¼ teaspoon hot sauce
Dash of pepper
1 cup crushed corn flakes

Combine all ingredients except corn flakes. Shape mixture into 1-inch balls; coat with crushed corn flakes. Place on lightly greased baking sheets; bake at 350° for 30 minutes. Serve warm. Yield: 2 dozen.

HOLIDAY PASTRY SWIRLS

1 large green pepper
1 large sweet red pepper
2 tablespoons sesame seeds, toasted
2 cups all-purpose flour
1 cup grated Parmesan cheese
½ teaspoon red pepper
¾ cup butter
⅓ cup water

Place whole peppers on their sides on a baking sheet. Bake at 500° for 20 minutes or until skin is blackened and charred. Transfer peppers immediately to a paper bag, and seal the top. Refrigerate 10 minutes or until peppers cool. Peel and seed peppers, discarding seeds and charred skin. Chop peppers finely; press between paper towels to remove excess moisture. Combine peppers and sesame seeds; set aside.

Combine flour, cheese, and red pepper; cut in butter with a pastry blender until mixture resembles coarse meal. Sprinkle water evenly over surface; stir with a fork until dry ingredients are moistened. Shape into 4 balls; cover and chill.

Roll each ball of dough into a 10- x 7-inch rectangle on a lightly floured surface. Sprinkle dough with one-fourth of pepper mixture. Roll dough jellyroll fashion, beginning with long end. Seal edges; wrap roll in wax paper, and chill at least 1 hour. Repeat procedure with remaining dough and pepper mixture.

Cut each roll into ¼-inch slices. Place on lightly greased baking sheets, and bake at 400° for 11 to 12 minutes or until edges are lightly browned. Cool on wire racks. Yield: 6½ dozen.

Note: To make ahead, freeze rolls in an airtight container up to 1 month. Thaw slightly; slice and bake as directed above.

Gift Ideas

CITRUS FRUIT SALAD DRESSING

1 (6-ounce) can frozen limeade
    concentrate, thawed and undiluted
⅓ cup vegetable oil
⅓ cup honey
2 teaspoons poppy seeds

Combine all ingredients in container of an electric blender; process until well blended. Pour mixture into a bottle; refrigerate up to 1 month. Yield: 1½ cups.

Directions for gift card: Store Citrus Fruit Salad Dressing in refrigerator up to 1 month. Shake dressing just before serving, and drizzle over fresh fruit.

NEW YEAR'S DAY CHILI MIX

1 (16-ounce) package dried kidney
    beans
1 tablespoon instant minced onion
2 teaspoons beef-flavored bouillon
    granules
1 teaspoon salt
½ teaspoon garlic powder
2½ tablespoons chili powder
1 teaspoon dried whole oregano
¼ teaspoon red pepper
1 small bay leaf

Place beans in an airtight plastic bag; set aside. Combine instant minced onion and next 3 ingredients; place in a small airtight plastic bag and, if desired, in a decorative paper bag, and label "Flavoring Packet."

Combine chili powder and remaining ingredients; place in a small airtight plastic bag, and, if desired, in a decorative paper bag, and label "Seasoning Packet." Yield: 1 (3-bag) gift.

Directions for gift recipe card: Sort and wash beans; place in a large Dutch oven.

Cover with water 2 inches above beans; let soak 8 hours. Drain.

Combine beans, Flavoring Packet, and 7 cups water in a large Dutch oven. Bring to a boil; cover, reduce heat, and simmer 1 hour, stirring occasionally.

Stir in 1 pound ground beef, cooked and drained, 1 (8-ounce) can tomato sauce, 1 (6-ounce) can tomato paste, and Seasoning Packet. Bring to a boil; reduce heat and simmer, uncovered, 30 minutes, stirring occasionally. Remove bay leaf. Yield: 11 cups.

Above: Ease "bowl day" meal preparation with a gift of New Year's Day Chili Mix.

Above: Make batches of Chocolate-Almond Spread for a bounty of delicious gifts.

CHOCOLATE-ALMOND SPREAD

   1 (12-ounce) package semisweet
      chocolate morsels
  ⅓ cup light corn syrup
  ⅓ cup whipping cream
   1 teaspoon chocolate almondine extract
      or almond extract
  ½ cup chopped almonds, toasted

Combine chocolate morsels, corn syrup, and whipping cream in top of a double boiler; bring water to a boil. Reduce heat to low, and cook until chocolate melts, stirring occasionally. Remove from heat, and stir in extract and almonds. Spoon into two 1-cup containers, and refrigerate for up to 1 month. Yield: about 2 cups.

Directions for gift card: Store Chocolate-Almond Spread in refrigerator up to 1 month. Serve with cookies, croissants, or fruit.

SPICED COFFEE MIX

  ½ cup instant coffee granules
  ¼ cup firmly packed brown sugar
  ¼ teaspoon ground cinnamon
  ¼ teaspoon ground cloves
  ¼ teaspoon ground nutmeg

138

Combine all ingredients, stirring well. Store at room temperature in an airtight container. Yield: ¾ cup. (12 servings.)

Directions for gift recipe card: Combine 1 tablespoon coffee mix and 1 cup boiling water.

For Swedish coffee, add a strip of orange rind to 1 cup coffee; top with whipped cream.

For Mexican coffee, add 2 teaspoons chocolate syrup and ⅛ teaspoon ground cinnamon to 1 cup coffee; top with whipped cream.

For Turkish coffee, add 1 teaspoon honey or sugar and 1 crushed cardamom seed to 1 cup coffee; top with whipped cream.

CINNAMON-NUT COFFEE CAKE MIX

  2 cups self-rising flour
  1 cup firmly packed brown sugar
  ⅓ cup quick-cooking oats
  3 tablespoons cultured buttermilk powder
  1 teaspoon ground cinnamon
  ¼ teaspoon ground nutmeg
  ½ cup butter-flavored shortening

Combine first 6 ingredients. Cut in shortening with a pastry blender until mixture resembles coarse meal. Spoon mixture into an airtight plastic bag, and label "Coffee Cake Mix"; store in a cool, dry place or in refrigerator up to 6 weeks. Yield: 1 gift package.

Topping Mixture:

  ¼ cup graham cracker crumbs
  2 tablespoons brown sugar
  ¼ teaspoon ground cinnamon
  ¼ cup chopped pecans

Combine all ingredients; seal in airtight plastic bag, and label "Topping Mixture." Store in a cool, dry place or in refrigerator up to 6 weeks. Yield: topping for 1 coffee cake gift package.

Directions for gift recipe card: Store the Cinnamon-Nut Coffee Cake Mix in a cool, dry place or in refrigerator up to 6 weeks. To prepare, combine Coffee Cake Mix, 2 eggs, and 1 cup water, stirring just until moistened. Pour mixture into a lightly greased 9-inch square pan. Sprinkle with Topping Mixture. Bake at 350° for 30 to 35 minutes or until a wooden pick inserted in center comes out clean. Yield: 9 servings.

ALMOND-ORANGE BREAD MIX

  2 cups all-purpose flour
  1 cup sugar
  2½ tablespoons instant nonfat dry milk powder
  2 teaspoons baking powder
  ½ teaspoon salt
  2 teaspoons dehydrated orange peel
  ⅓ cup butter-flavored shortening
  1 (2-ounce) package slivered almonds, toasted and chopped

Combine first 6 ingredients; cut in shortening with a pastry blender until the mixture resembles coarse meal. Stir in almonds. Store mixture in an airtight container at room temperature up to 6 weeks. Refrigerate for longer storage. Yield: one 3½-cup gift package.

Directions for gift recipe card: Store the Almond-Orange Bread Mix at room temperature up to 6 weeks, or refrigerate for longer storage. To prepare, beat 1 (8-ounce) package cream cheese, softened, until light and fluffy. Add 2 eggs, one at a time, beating after each addition. Stir in ½ cup water, ½ teaspoon almond extract, and package of bread mix. Spoon batter into a greased 9- x 5- x 3-inch loafpan. Bake at 325° for 55 minutes or until a wooden pick inserted in center comes out clean. Cool in pan 10 minutes; remove from pan, and cool on a wire rack. Serve with cherry jam, if desired. Yield: 1 loaf.

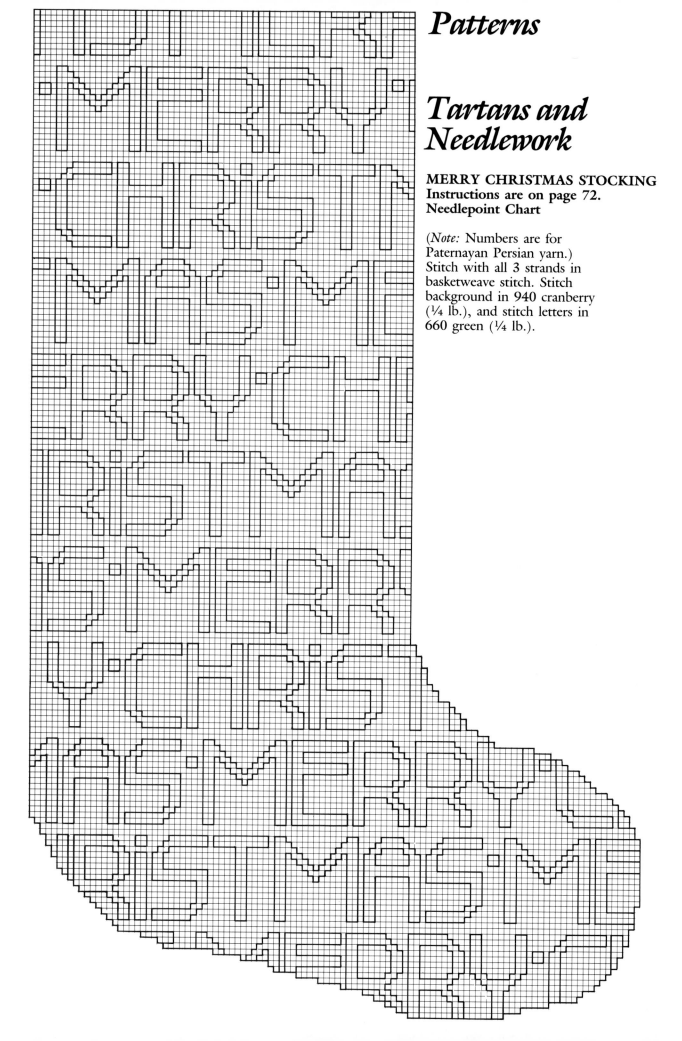

Patterns

Tartans and Needlework

MERRY CHRISTMAS STOCKING
Instructions are on page 72.
Needlepoint Chart

(*Note:* Numbers are for Paternayan Persian yarn.) Stitch with all 3 strands in basketweave stitch. Stitch background in 940 cranberry (¼ lb.), and stitch letters in 660 green (¼ lb.).

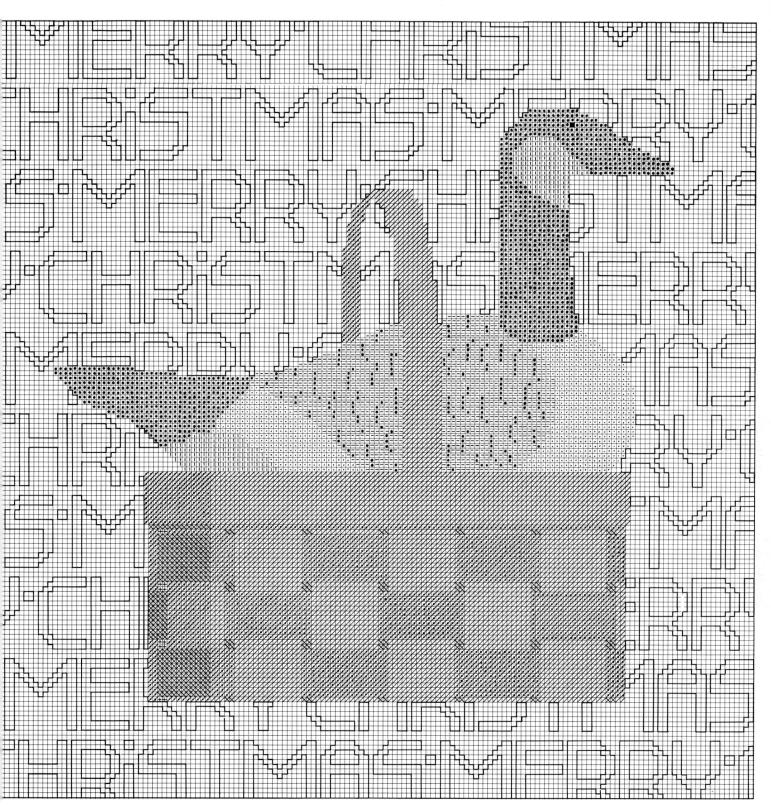

MERRY CHRISTMAS GOOSE
Instructions are on page 72.
Needlepoint Chart

COLOR KEY
(*Note:* Numbers are for Paternayan Persian yarn.)
Stitch with all 3 strands in basketweave stitch. For eye,
stitch a double French knot with all 3 strands in black.
Stitch background in 940 cranberry (¼ lb.), and stitch
letters in 660 green (¼ lb.).

•	220	Black	½ oz.
ı	260	White	½ oz.
·	201	Gray	½ oz.
✕	871	Rust	½ oz.
+	410	Dark Brown	8 yd. twist
╱	424	Tan	½ oz.
╱	405	Light Tan	½ oz.
−	463	Light Brown	½ oz.

141

Set the Table

Instructions are on page 97.
Patterns are full-size and include
⅛″ seam allowance.

Place Mat:
Cut 3 hearts from red print.

Table Runner:
Cut 4 hearts from red print #1.
Cut 6 birds from red print #2.
Cut 6 wings from green print #1.
Cut 8 trees from green print #2.

Chair Back:
Cut 3 hearts from red print #1.
Cut 1 bird from red print #2,
reverse and cut 1 more.
Cut 1 wing from green print
#1, reverse and cut 1 more.
Cut 3 trees from green
print #2.

TREE

Cutting Line

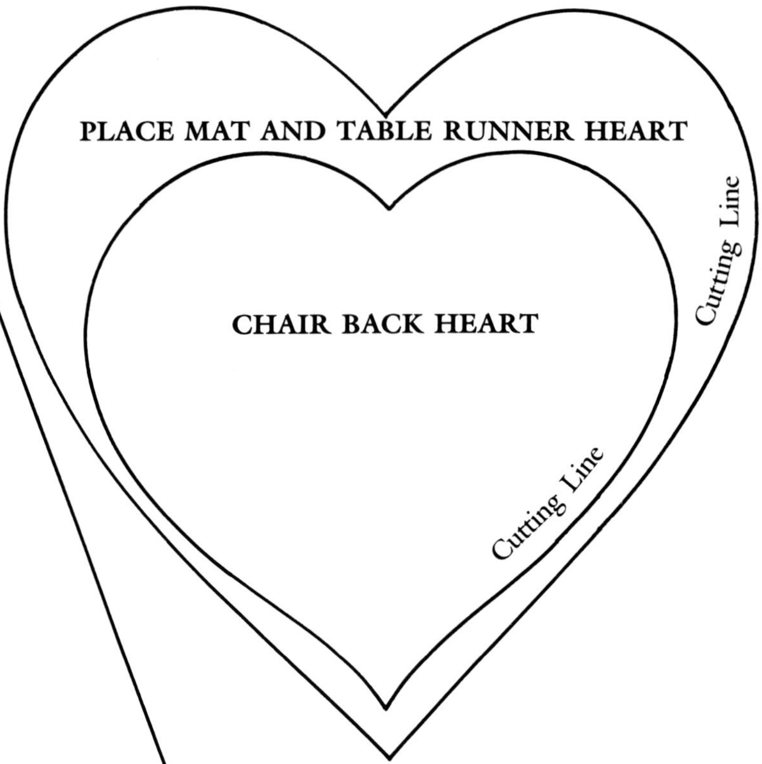

PLACE MAT AND TABLE RUNNER HEART

CHAIR BACK HEART

Cutting Line

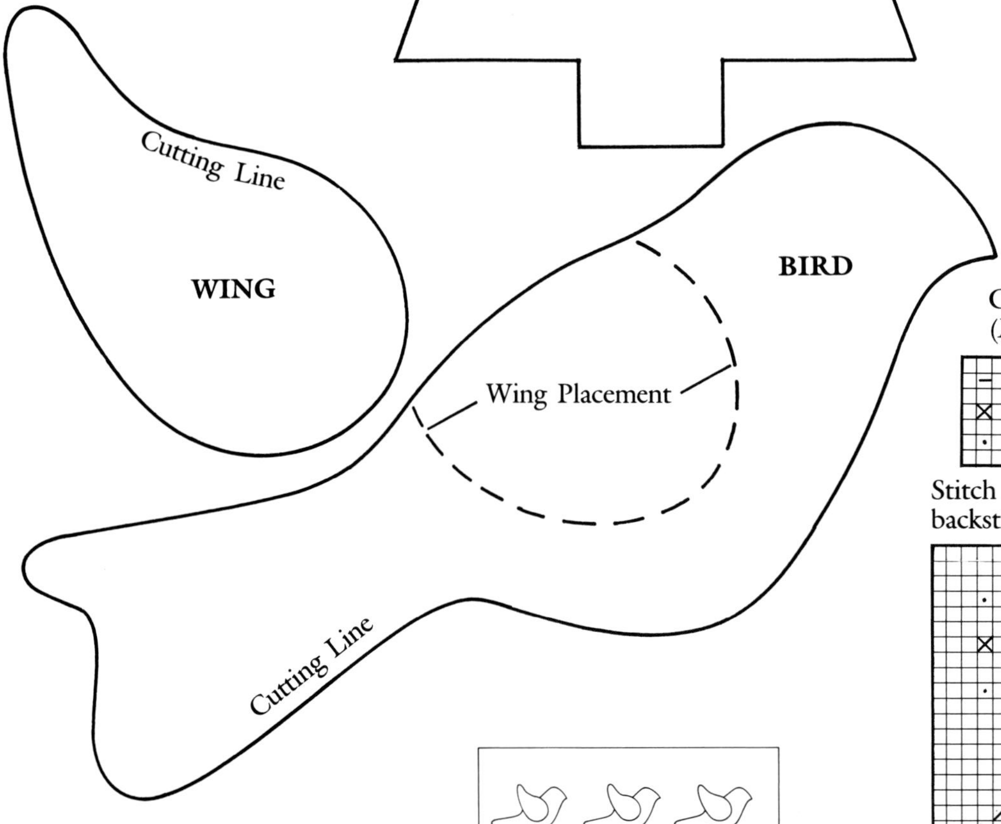

Cutting Line

Cutting Line

Cutting Line

WING

BIRD

Wing Placement

Cutting Line

Cross-Stitch Ornaments

LOG CARRIER
Instructions are on page 82.
Cross-Stitch Chart

COLOR KEY
(*Note:* Numbers are for DMC floss.)

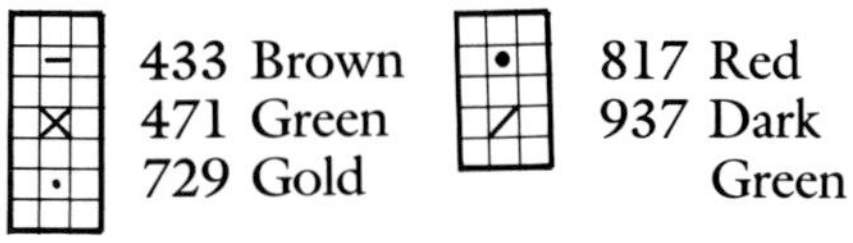

− 433 Brown	• 817 Red
× 471 Green	/ 937 Dark
729 Gold	Green

Stitch with 2 strands. With 1 strand,
backstitch letters in red.

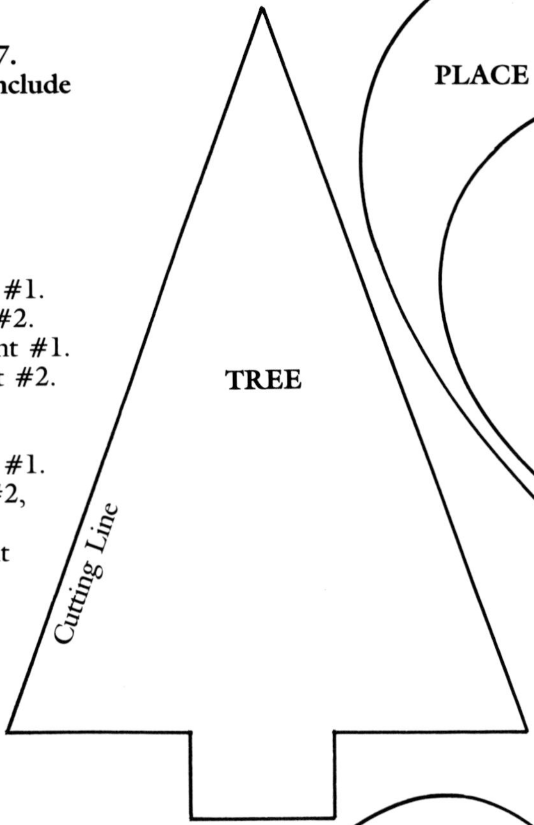

**Diagram—Table Runner
Appliqué Placement**

142

Center

ALL HEARTS
COME HOME FOR
CHRISTMAS

Center

Tartans and Needlework

PICTURE FRAME
Instructions are on page 75. Pattern is full-size.

Diagram—Oval Placement and Fold Stitching Line

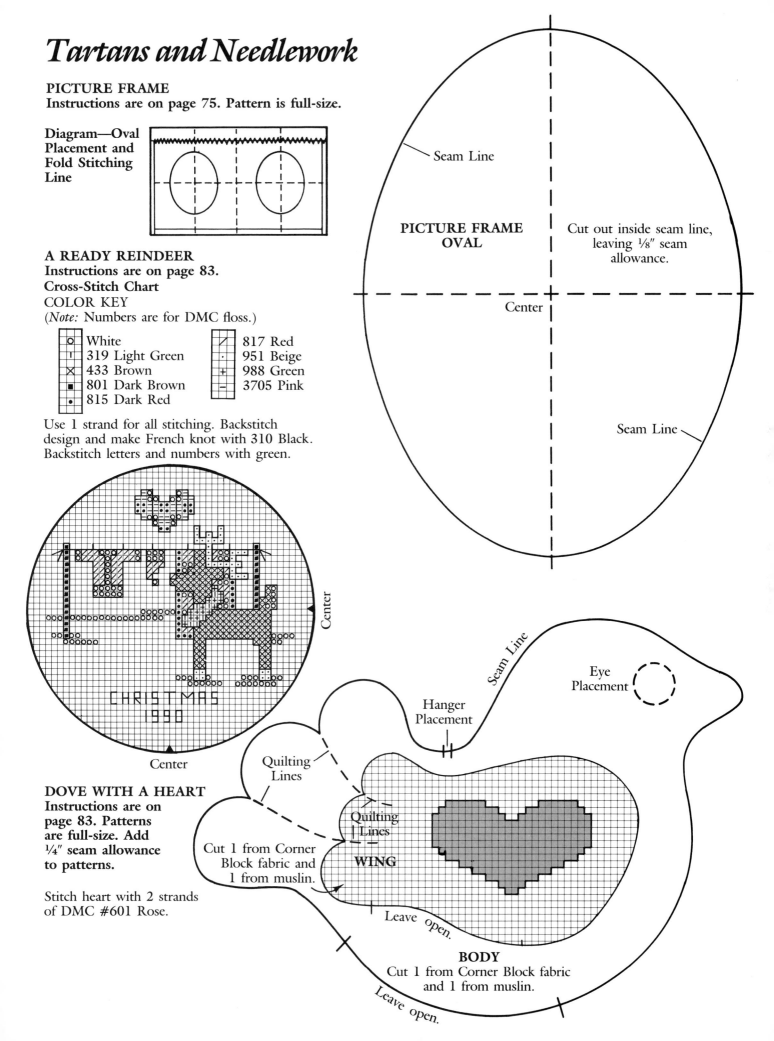

A READY REINDEER
Instructions are on page 83.
Cross-Stitch Chart
COLOR KEY
(*Note:* Numbers are for DMC floss.)

○	White	╱	817	Red
!	319 Light Green	·	951	Beige
✕	433 Brown	+	988	Green
■	801 Dark Brown	−	3705	Pink
•	815 Dark Red			

Use 1 strand for all stitching. Backstitch design and make French knot with 310 Black. Backstitch letters and numbers with green.

CHRISTMAS
1990

Center

Center

DOVE WITH A HEART
Instructions are on page 83. Patterns are full-size. Add ¼″ seam allowance to patterns.

Stitch heart with 2 strands of DMC #601 Rose.

PICTURE FRAME OVAL

Seam Line

Cut out inside seam line, leaving ⅛″ seam allowance.

Center

Seam Line

Seam Line

Eye Placement

Hanger Placement

Quilting Lines

Quilting Lines

WING

Cut 1 from Corner Block fabric and 1 from muslin.

Leave open.

BODY
Cut 1 from Corner Block fabric and 1 from muslin.

Leave open.

Friends Gather to Quilt

LITTLE CABIN
Instructions are on page 86.
Patterns are full-size. Add ¼″ seam allowance
to all pattern pieces.

Diagram—Quilt Assembly

I
(Ornament)

1

2

3

4

5

6

H

A
(Pillow)

A

A
(Pillow)

H

F
(Pillow)

E

A

B

A

B

C

D

C

A

welcome

G

7 Pillow

7 Ornament

From the pattern "Cabins,"
©1986 The Little Quilt Collection

Stitch a Classic Sampler Pillow

Instructions are on page 79.
Cross-Stitch Chart

Center

Center

COLOR KEY

320 Light Green	517 Blue
350 Coral	519 Light Blue
353 Peach	611 Brown
433 Dark Brown	816 Dark Red
501 Blue-green	

(*Note:* All numbers are for DMC floss.)
Use 2 strands for all stitching. Backstitch houses
and large hearts with 2 strands of 3371
black-brown.

Top

Tartans and Needlework

PARTY CUMMERBUND
Instructions are on page 77.
Patterns are full-size and
include ¼″ seam allowance.

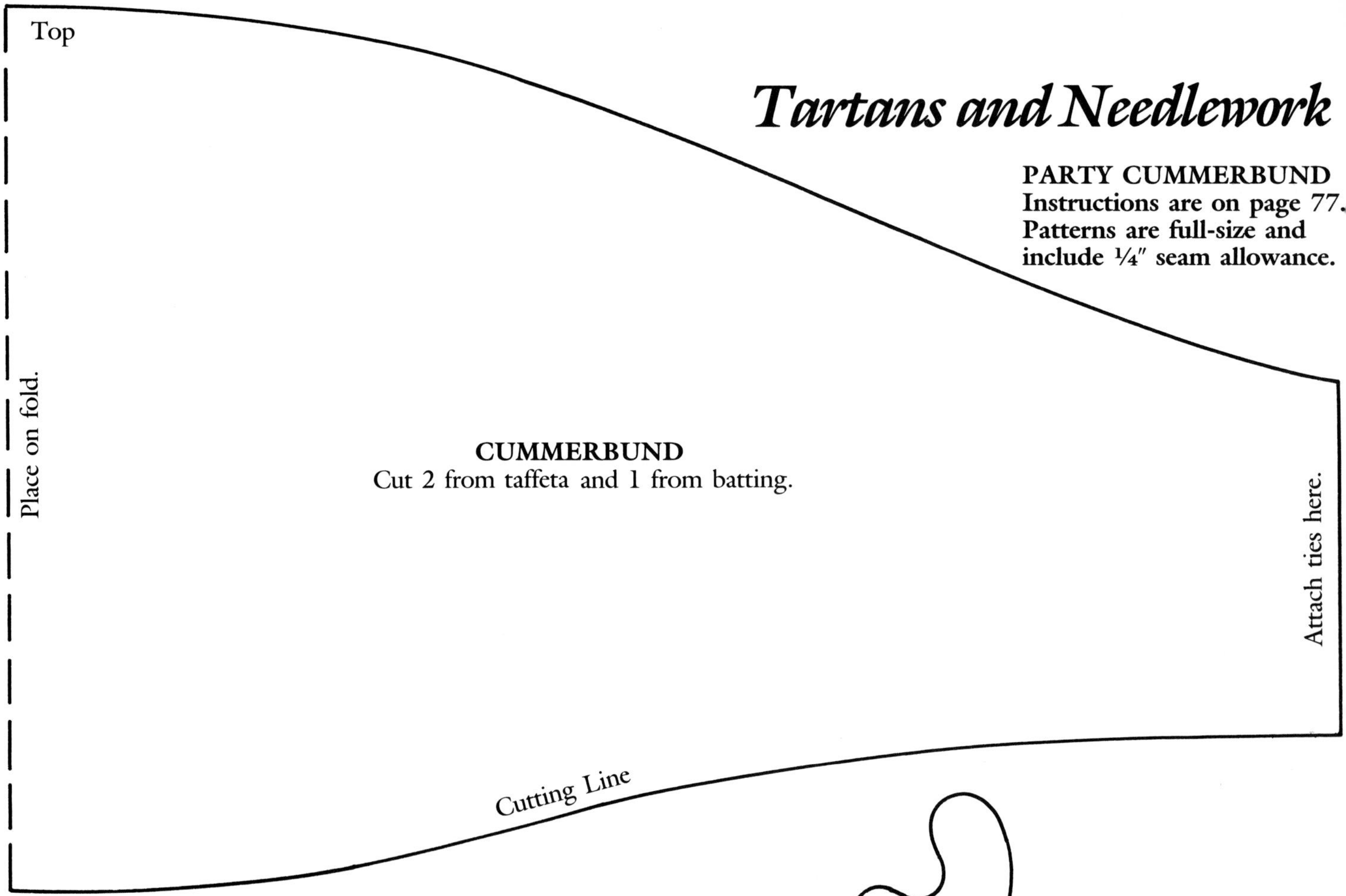

Place on fold.

CUMMERBUND
Cut 2 from taffeta and 1 from batting.

Attach ties here.

Cutting Line

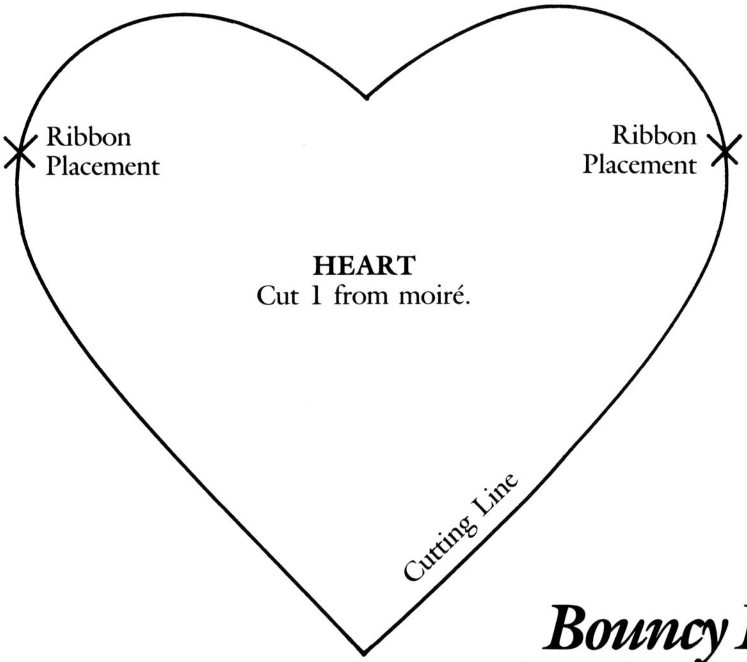

Ribbon
Placement

Ribbon
Placement

◯ Eye Placement

HEART
Cut 1 from moiré.

Cutting Line

Seam Line

Bouncy Little Reindeer

Instructions are on page 81.
Pattern is full-size.

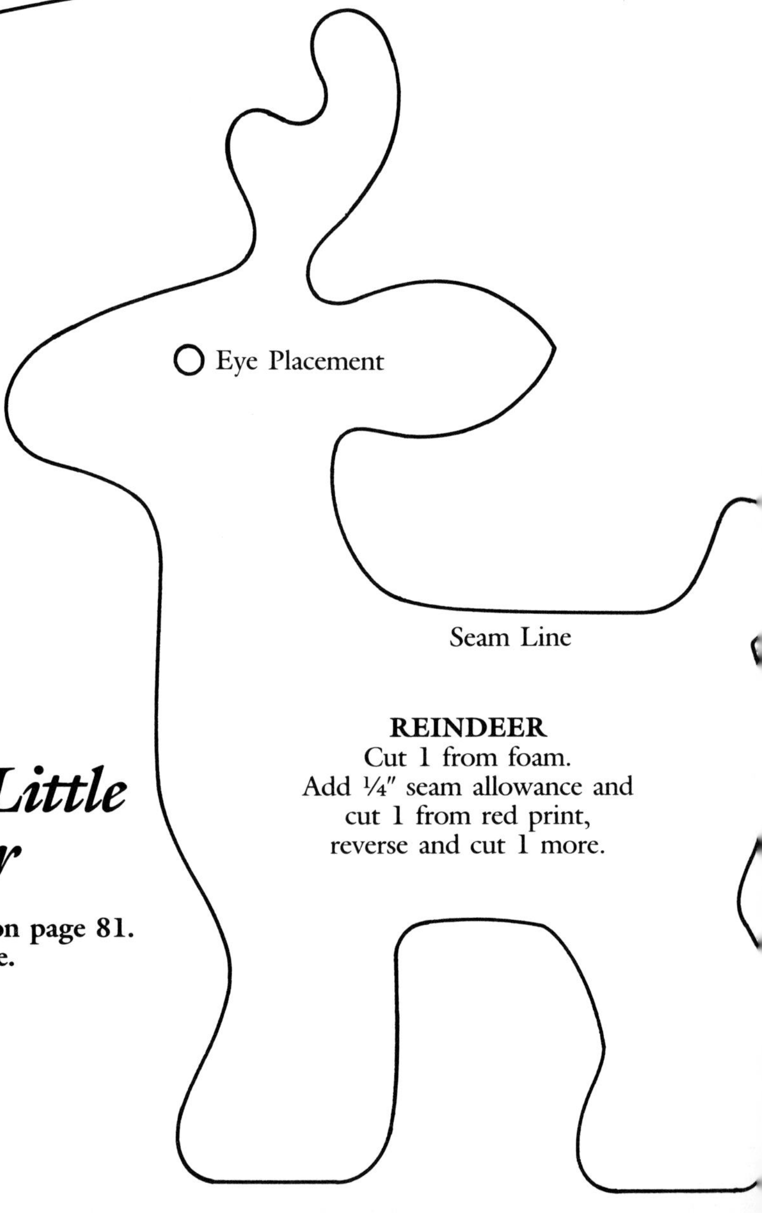

REINDEER
Cut 1 from foam.
Add ¼″ seam allowance and
cut 1 from red print,
reverse and cut 1 more.

Knitted Snowflakes and Trees

Instructions are on page 89.
Duplicate-Stitch Chart—Snowflakes

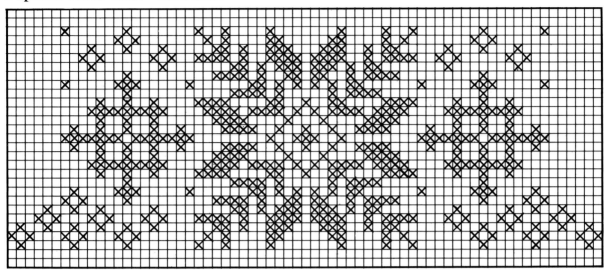

Duplicate-Stitch Chart—Tree

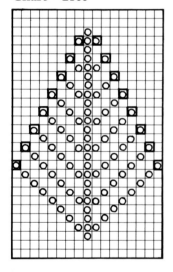

Knitting Chart—Leaves

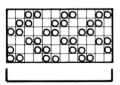

Repeat

COLOR KEY

Green
Red

Start Something Cooking

GREEN QUILTED APRON
Instructions are on page 92.
Diagram—Cutting and Assembly Guide

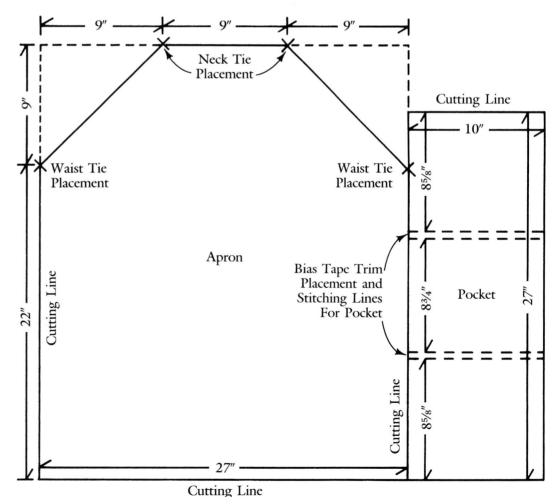

Start Something Cooking

SNOWMAN APRON
Instructions are on page 94.
Patterns are full-size and include ¼" seam allowance.

**Diagram—Pattern Assembly
and Appliqué Placement**

✕ Neck Strap
Placement

Cutting Line

Place on fold.

Machine satin-stitch
eyebrows.

SNOWMAN
Cut 1 from white, Christmas
print, and batting.

Eye
Placement

CHEEK
Cut 2 from red pindot.

NOSE
Cut 1 from
orange pindot.

Machine
satin-stitch mouth.

Match dots and continue pattern.

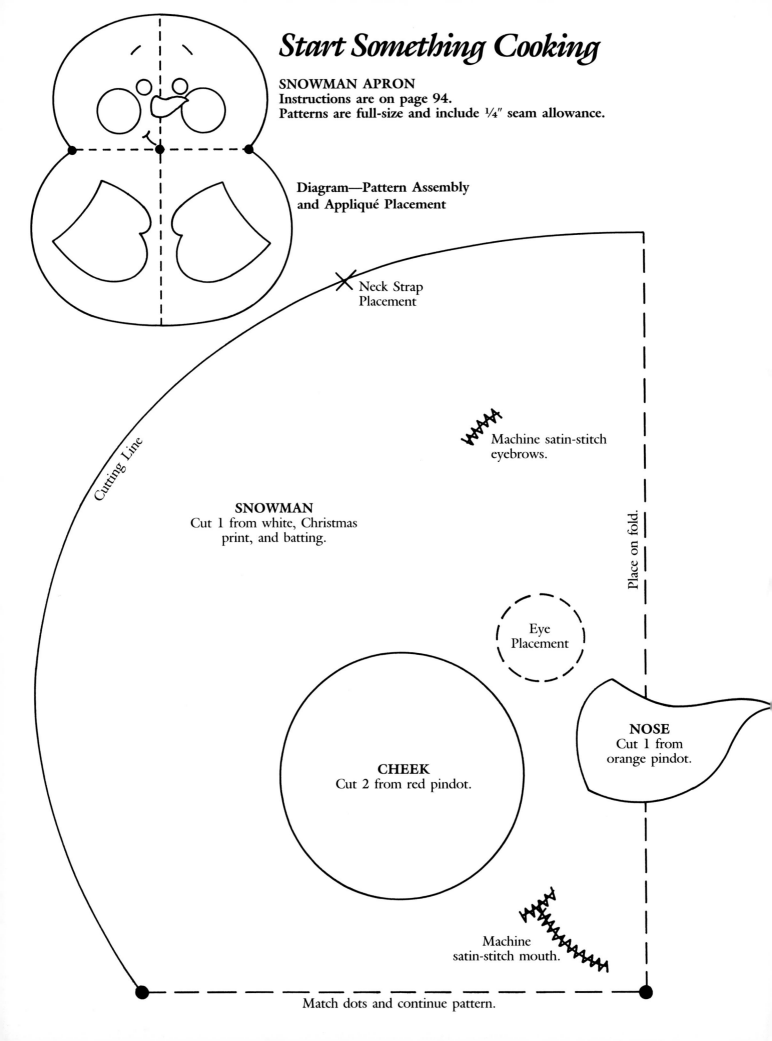

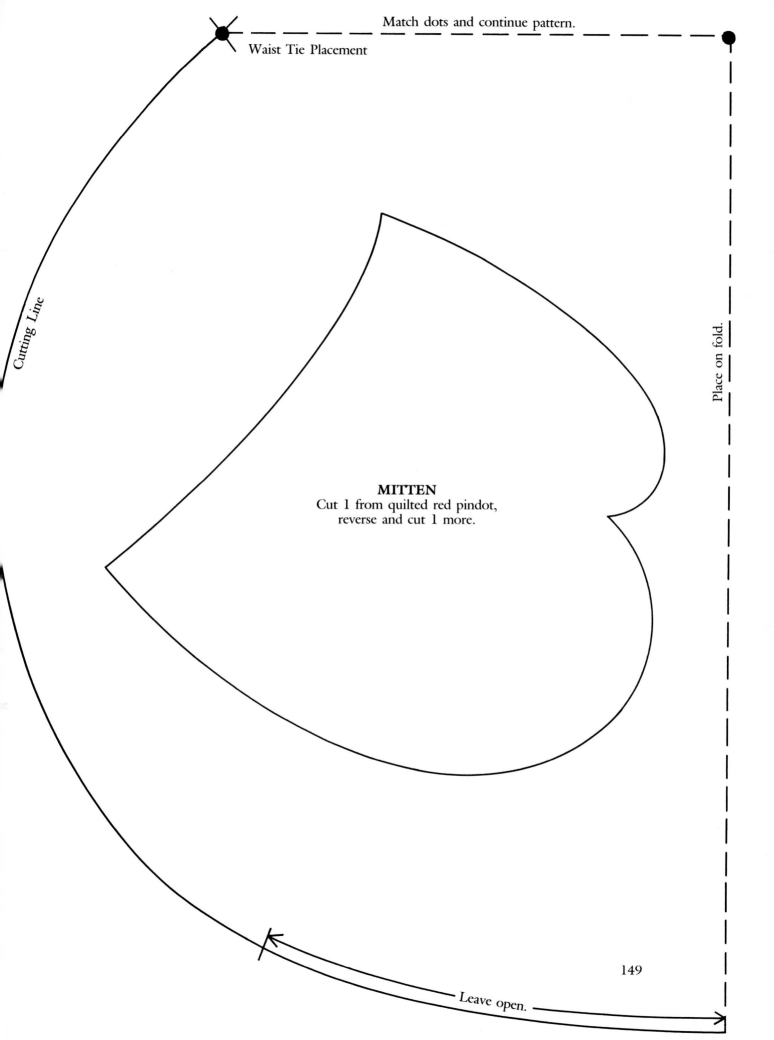

Match dots and continue pattern.

Waist Tie Placement

Cutting Line

Place on fold.

MITTEN
Cut 1 from quilted red pindot,
reverse and cut 1 more.

149

Leave open.

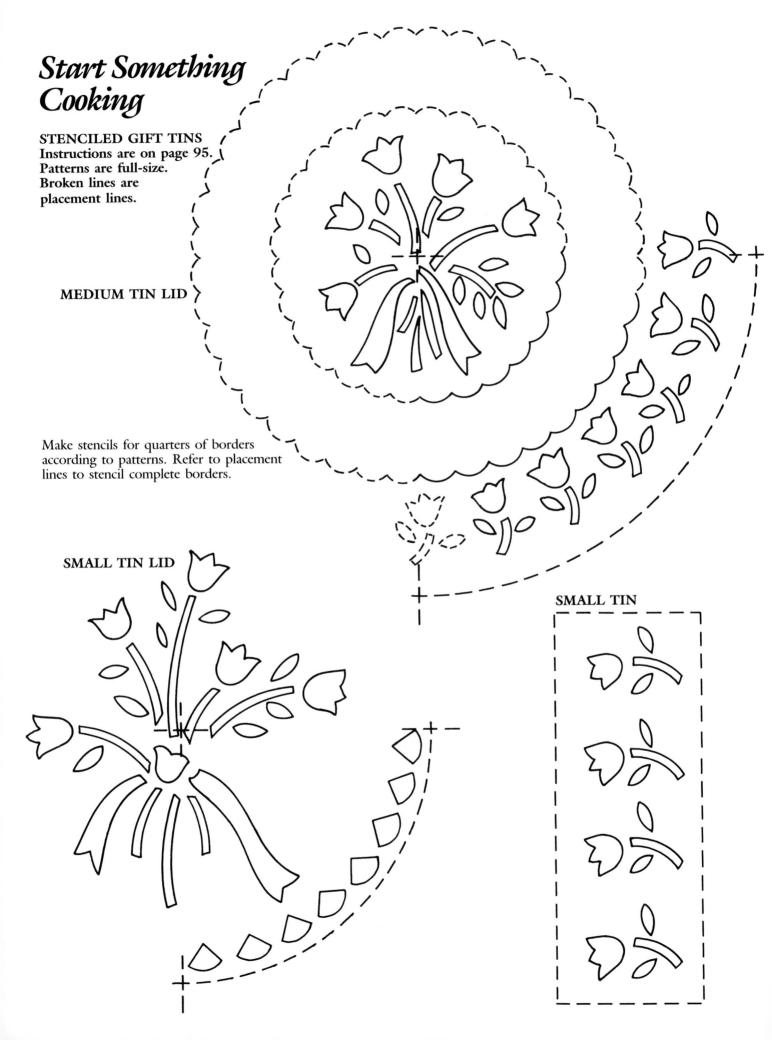

Start Something Cooking

STENCILED GIFT TINS
Instructions are on page 95.
Patterns are full-size.
Broken lines are
placement lines.

MEDIUM TIN LID

Make stencils for quarters of borders
according to patterns. Refer to placement
lines to stencil complete borders.

SMALL TIN LID

SMALL TIN

Center on tin.

Carousel Stocking

Instructions are on page 91.   **Cross-Stitch Chart**   Use last line of verse to position words above hors

just once a year

▲
Center

Cross-Stitch Chart

COLOR KEY
(*Note:* Numbers are for DMC floss.)

White	
310 Black	
321 Red	
413 Dark Gray	
414 Medium Gray	
415 Light Gray	
434 Light Brown	
801 Dark Brown	
700 Green	
725 Yellow	
Gold*	
815 Dark Red	

*Gold (1 strand 725 Yellow and 2 strands Balger gold blending filament)

Stitch with 2 strands except for areas marked gold (refer to color key). Backstitch lowercase letters with 2 strands green and horse with 1 strand black.

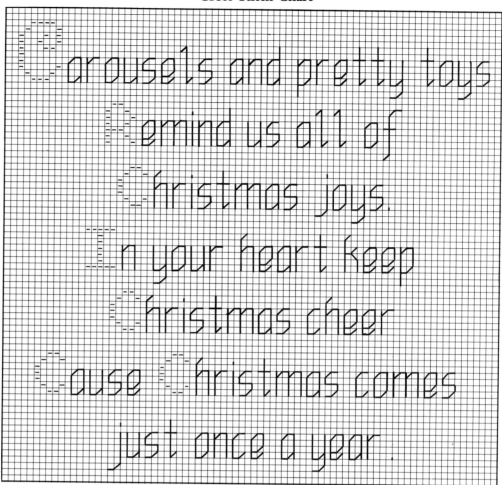

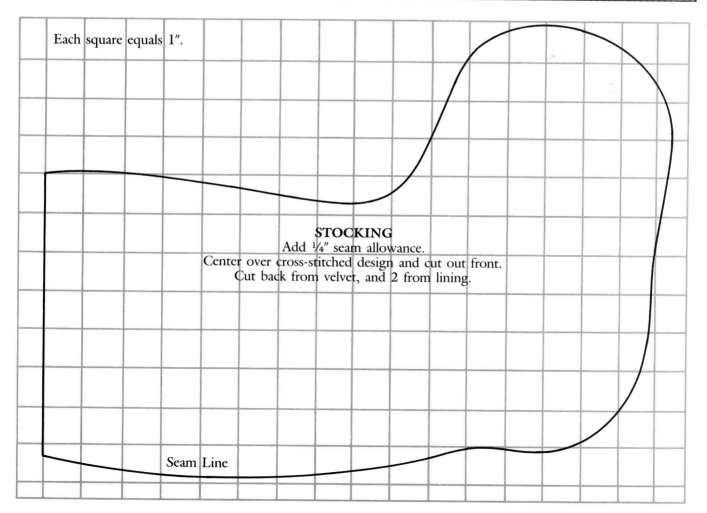

Each square equals 1″.

STOCKING
Add ¼″ seam allowance.
Center over cross-stitched design and cut out front.
Cut back from velvet, and 2 from lining.

Seam Line

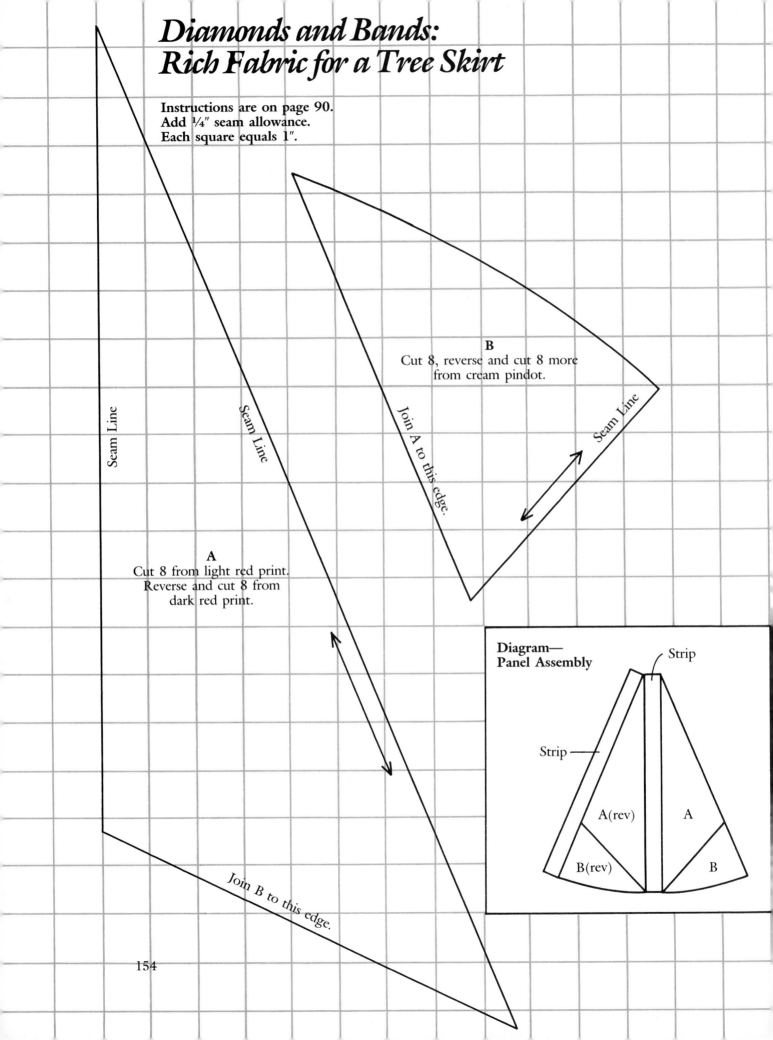

Diamonds and Bands:
Rich Fabric for a Tree Skirt

Instructions are on page 90.
Add ¼" seam allowance.
Each square equals 1".

Seam Line

Seam Line

B
Cut 8, reverse and cut 8 more
from cream pindot.

Join A to this edge.

Seam Line

A
Cut 8 from light red print.
Reverse and cut 8 from
dark red print.

Join B to this edge.

154

**Diagram—
Panel Assembly**

Strip

Strip

A(rev)

A

B(rev)

B

Tartans and Needlework

CHRISTMAS KITTEN SWEATER
Instructions are on page 76.

Knitting Chart
Work background in red, kitten in white,
wreath in green, and bow in yellow.

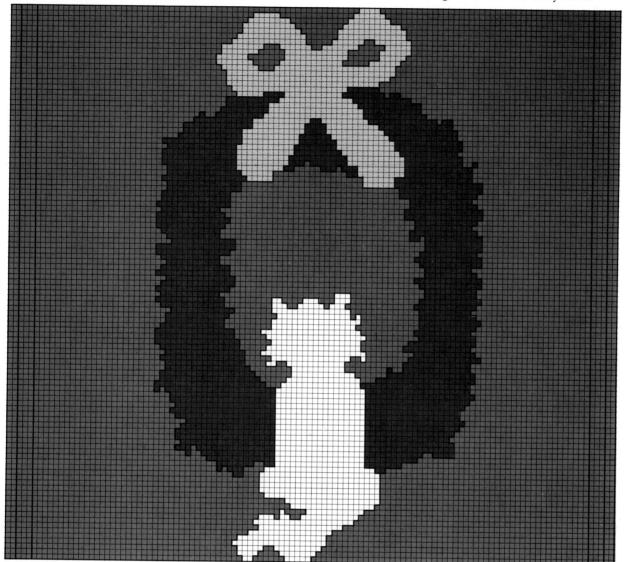

L M S   S M L

Resources

To order the Colonial Williamsburg catalog mentioned on pages 10-11 and 60-61, write Colonial Williamsburg, P.O. Box CH, Williamsburg, VA 23187, or call 1-800-446-9240.

For information about the Orchard Inn (see page 13), call 704/749-5471 or write The Orchard Inn, P.O. Box 725, Saluda, NC 28773.

To order a catalog of wire topiary forms (see page 24), write Topiary, Inc., 41 Bering Street, Tampa, FL 33606.

Mary Lois Forbes's shop (see pages 26-29), Visions of Sugarplums, 3815 Clairmont Avenue, Birmingham, AL 35222, is open Tuesday through Saturday 11 a.m. to 6 p.m. For more information call 205/592-9004.

The Nancy Thomas Gallery (see pages 32-35), 145 Ballard Street, Yorktown, VA 23690 is open Tuesday through Saturday 10 a.m. to 4 p.m. and Sunday 1 to 4 p.m. Nancy's work is also available by mail order, 804/898-3665.

For a catalog of Santa chocolate molds (see pages 36 and 37), write the Holcraft Collection, P.O. Box 792, Davis, CA 95616, or call 916/756-3023.

To order patterns for the six stockings shown on page 42, send $5 and your name and address to Suzanne McNeill, 401 N. Bailey-SL, Ft. Worth, TX 76107.

To order the crystal and Santa ornament vases shown on pages 56-58, write Dorothy McDaniel's, Inc., Attention: Mail Order, P.O. Box 59641, Birmingham, AL 35259, or call 205/871-0092.

Contributors

DESIGNERS

Jeffrey K. Adkisson, stairway arrangement, 57.
Kathryn Marshall Arnold and Jane Davies (for the Craft House, Colonial Williamsburg Foundation), crystalline table, 60.
Curtis Boehringer, stocking, 72; goose picture, 72; piano bench cushion, 80.
Georgia Bonesteel, folded fabric box, 71.
Carolyn Caswell, toys, 66; tree, 67.
Lyn Cutler, mantel arrangement, bottom 59.
Marilyn Dorwart, appliquéd table set, 96.
Dixie L. Falls, knitted tree skirt, 89.
Sandra Lounsbury Foose, foam reindeer, 81; quilted apron, 92.
Joyce M. Gillis, snowman apron, 94.
Bill Graham and Carolyn Caswell, marbleized balls, 68.
Werner Gross, cyclamen arrangement, 52.
June Hudson, wreath with bottles, left 56.
Little Quilts™, pillow, 86; ornament, 87.
Dorothy McDaniel, mantel garland, 58; table and buffet arrangements, 61.
Marilyn Michael, angel arrangement, top 59.
Margaret Allen Northen and Memory Hagler, kitten in wreath sweater, 76.
Carole Rodgers, carousel horse stocking, 91.
Judyth Smith, cummerbund, 77.
Catherine S. Stoddard, pillow slipcovers, 78; tapestry trees, 78.
Nan Tournier, diamond tree skirt, 90.
Lois Winston, sampler pillow, 79; log carrier ornament, 82; reindeer ornament, 83; dove ornament, 83.
Cecily H. Zerega, stenciled tins, 95.

PHOTOGRAPHERS

Van Chaplin, 14, 15, 16, 17, 18, 19, 20, 21, 40, 41, 42, 43, 44, 62, 63, 64, 65.
Gary Clark, 4, 5, 6, 7, 8, 9, 10, 11, 12, top 36, 37, 60, 77, 79.
Colleen Duffley, cover, title page, contents, 1, 2-3, 25, 45, 69, 99, 100, 101, 103, 104, 109, 110, 113, 115, 116, 119, 120, 123, 126, 129, 132, 135, 137, 138.
Mary-Gray Hunter, top 27, 53, top 59, 73, 74, right 78, 90, 92.
Sylvia Martin, bottom 52.
Art Meripol, 23.
John O'Hagan, 13, 30, right 31, 32, 33, 34, 35, bottom 36, 38, 39, top 52, 54, 55, left 56, 66, 67, 68, 70, 71, left 78, 80, 81, 83, 84, 85, 86, 87, 88, 91, 93, 94, 95.
Cheryl Sales, 58, 61.
Melissa Springer, 22, 24, 26, bottom 27, 28, 29, 46, 47, 48, 49, 50, 51, right 56, 57, bottom 59, 82, 96, 98.
Jan Wyatt, left 31.

PHOTOSTYLISTS

Leslie Byars, 100, 101, 103, 104, 109, 110, 113, 115, 116, 119, 120, 123, 126, 129, 132, 135, 137, 138.
Connie Formby, 96, 98.
Diane Burnett Lupo, top 52.
Catherine S. Stoddard, 26, 27, 28, 29, 73, 74, 78, 81, 82, 83, 84, 85, 88, 90, 93, 94, 95.

Special thanks to the *Southern Living* Test Kitchens staff for preparing recipes.

156